Japan,
the United States,
and
prospects for the
Asia-Pacific
century

Japan, the United States, and prospects for the Asia-Pacific century

three scenarios for the future

Richard P. Cronin

ST. MARTIN'S PRESS, NEW YORK

INSTITUTE OF SOUTHEAST ASIAN STUDIES, SINGAPORE

Published by
Institute of Southeast Asian Studies
Heng Mui Keng Terrace
Pasir Panjang
Singapore 0511

First published in the United States of America in 1992.
For information, write:
Scholarly and Reference Division, St. Martin's Press, Inc., 175 Fifth Avenue, New York, NY 10010

The responsibility for facts and opinions expressed in this publication rests exclusively with the author and his interpretations do not necessarily reflect the views or the policy of the Congressional Research Service, the Library of Congress, any other agency or department of the U.S. Government, and the Institute of Southeast Asian Studies or its supporters.

Library of Congress Cataloguing-in-Publication Data

Cronin, Richard P.
  Japan, the United States and prospects for the Asia-Pacific century: three scenarios for the future/Richard P. Cronin
  p.   cm.
  ISBN 0-312-08675-X
  1. Japan—History—1945-.
  2. Asia—Relations—Asia.
  3. Asia—Relations—Japan.
  4. Japan—Relations—Pacific Area.
  5. Pacific Area—Relations—Japan.
  6. United States—Foreign economic relations.
  I. Title.
DS889.C76   1992
952.04—dc20
                                                92-21918
                                                    CIP

ISBN 981-3016-22-1 (soft cover, ISEAS, Singapore)
ISBN 981-3016-23-x (hard cover, ISEAS, Singapore)
For the USA and Canada, this hard cover edition (ISBN 0-312-08675-X) is published by St. Martin's Press, New York.

Typeset by The Fototype
Printed in Singapore by

Contents

List of tables

List of tables

List of figures

Acknowledgements

This book is substantially the product of research undertaken while on leave of absence from the Congressional Research Service (CRS) of the U.S. Library of Congress as a research fellow at the Institute of Southeast Asian Studies. I am very grateful to the Institute of Southeast Asian Studies, and especially its Director, Professor K.S. Sandhu, for providing the opportunity to carry out research on this timely and important topic. I owe a great deal to the ISEAS staff and the community of scholars from four continents with whom I exchanged ideas, shared experiences and enjoyed fellowship and friendship.

The idea for the project emerged during brief trips to Taiwan, Indonesia, Malaysia, Singapore and Japan beginning in early 1988. After formulating a preliminary concept during the summer of 1989, I took up the subject in earnest during my October 1989–June 1990 fellowship at ISEAS. During this period I had the opportunity to travel to Japan and a number of other Asian countries, namely Hong Kong, Indonesia, Malaysia, Thailand and India, to collect more data and test my hypotheses.

In addition to Professor Sandhu and ISEAS, I am obligated to a number of other individuals, institutions and agencies, who directly or indirectly aided this research. These include my own service, which generously gave me leave of absence to pursue this valuable career development opportunity; the U.S. Information Agency, which sponsored me on a speaking tour in Japan; the Asia Foundation and its then field representative in Kuala Lumpur, Julio A. Andrews; E. Gene Smith, Director of the Library of Congress Field Office in Jakarta, Indonesia; and Hitoshi Matsuoka of the Japanese Institute for Domestic and International Studies.

After several years of research, one's intellectual debt to other toilers in the same or adjacent vineyards becomes increasingly heavy. A very short list would include Robert C. Orr, Jr., of the Stanford Program in Kyoto, whose published writing and network of contacts in Japan have served my own purposes very well, and my colleagues at CRS, Robert Sutter, Raymond Ahearn, and Larry Nowels who provided valuable insights and critical reviews. I also owe a debt to the anonymous readers of the original manuscript for their thoughtful comments and suggestions. One reader, in particular, took considerable pains to critique the draft and offer very helpful suggestions. None of these, of course, bear any responsibility for the findings of this book.

I also wish to express my appreciation for secretarial, research and graphics support provided by Kathleen McCarthy, of the CRS Foreign Affairs and National Defense Division; for graphics assistance from Paul Graney, also of CRS; and for research assistance provided by Perry Bechky, a CRS student volunteer intern, during the initial phase of this project in the summer of 1989.

Finally, I would be remiss not to mention my deep appreciation for the support and forbearance of my wife, Nancy, and my children, Kate and Andrew, who allowed me to uproot them for nine months and install them in a new and sometimes trying situation half way around the world. I am conscious of the fact that while the adventure of living and travelling in Asia was a positive one for all of us, the overall balance of benefits and costs was less favourable in their case than in mine.

Japan in the Asia-Pacific Region

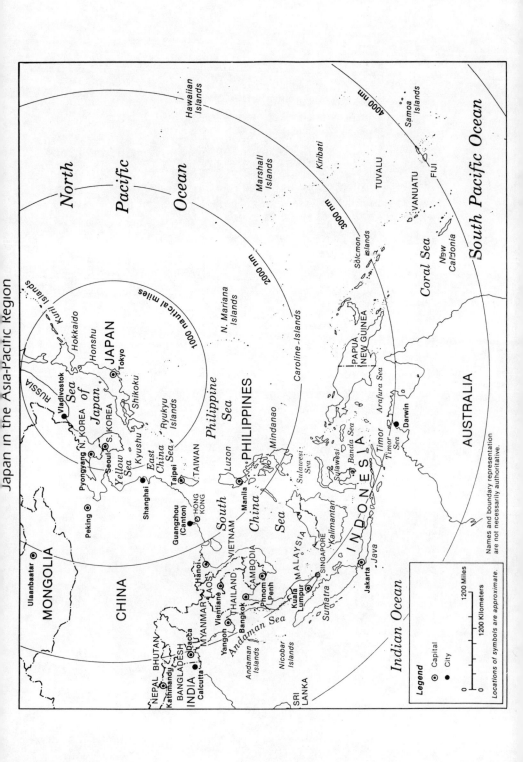

North

Pacific

Ocean

Hawaiian
Islands

Kuril Islands

RUSSIA

Hokkaido

Vladivostok

Honshu

JAPAN

Tokyo

Pyongyang

N. KOREA

Sea
of
Japan

Shikoku

Marshall
Islands

Kiribati

Samoa
Islands

TUVALU

VANUATU

FIJI

New
Caledonia

South Pacific Ocean

Coral Sea

Peking

Seoul

S. KOREA

Kyushu

Ryukyu
Islands

Yellow
Sea

East
China
Sea

Shanghai

Taipei

TAIWAN

Philippine
Sea

N. Mariana
Islands

Caroline Islands

Solomon
Islands

PAPUA
NEW GUINEA

Ulaanbaatar

MONGOLIA

Guangzhou
(Canton)

HONG
KONG

South
China
Sea

Luzon

PHILIPPINES

Manila

1000 nautical miles

2000 nm

3000 nm

4000 nm

CHINA

VIETNAM

Hanoi

LAOS

Vientiane

THAILAND

Bangkok

CAMBODIA

Phnom
Penh

Kuala
Lumpur

MALAYSIA

SINGAPORE

Mindanao

Sulawesi
Sea

Sulawesi

Kalimantan

INDONESIA

Banda Sea

Arafura Sea

Timor

Timor
Sea

Darwin

AUSTRALIA

NEPAL

BHUTAN

Kathmandu

INDIA

BANGLADESH

Dacca

Calcutta

MYANMAR

Yangon

Andaman
Islands

Andaman Sea

Nicobar
Islands

SRI
LANKA

Sumatra

Java

Jakarta

Indian Ocean

Names and boundary representation
are not necessarily authoritative.

Legend

◎ Capital

● City

0   1200 Miles

0   1200 Kilometers

Locations of symbols are approximate.

1
Shifting balance of power in the Asia-Pacific region

Based on recent trends, Japan in the decade of the 1990s will consolidate its position as the most important Asia-Pacific economic power, a development that likely will have highly significant consequences for future economic, political and security relationships. These include, especially, the respective roles and relative power of the United States and Japan. During the 1980s, Japan decisively displaced the United States as the largest source of new business investment and economic aid in the region stretching from South Asia to the Pacific islands (Table 1.1).[1]

As a consequence of the rapid expansion of its offshore manufacturing base, especially since the sharp rise in the value of the yen against the U.S. dollar following the September 1985 Plaza Accord, Japan has emerged as the region's "core economy" and the main catalyst of growing intra-regional trade. Although the United States remains a major factor in Asia-Pacific economic dynamism as a continuing source of business investment and technology, and the single largest market for the region's growing manufactured exports, Asia-Pacific countries increasingly look to Japan as the regional leader.

Many see Japan as having acquired peacefully much of the economic power and influence it sought unsuccessfully to gain by force of arms in World War II. Although there is increasing evidence of some serious underlying financial weaknesses in the Japanese economy, signified

Table 1.1
Aggregate indicators of U.S. and
Japanese economic involvement in the
Asia-Pacific region, 1980 and 1990
(In US$ billions)

	1980		1990	
	U.S.	Japan	U.S.	Japan
Direct Investment*				
Cumulative	16.7	9.8	42.4	65.6
Most recent year			(11.2)	(6.7)
Annual Bilateral Aid**	1.3	1.4	1.6	4.1
Economic Aid	1.0	1.4	1.2	4.1
Security Aid	0.3	0.0	0.4	0.0
Two Way Trade***	66.7	85.6	175.0	180.5
Exports to Asia-Pacific	32.3	40.8	70.5	98.2
Imports from Asia-Pacific	34.4	44.9	104.6	82.3
Total	84.7	96.8	219.0	250.2

* Investment comparisons should be used with great caution, if at all, due to methodological limitations of the data (Appendix A). U.S. investment data is on a calendar year, *equity position* basis, while Japanese data covers investment *approvals* in the fiscal year ending 31 March (i.e. 1990 data is for the period ending 31 March 1991).

** U.S. aid data is for the fiscal year beginning 1 October of the previous calendar year (FY 1990 begins 1 October 1989), while Japanese aid data is for the fiscal year beginning 1 April of the current calendar year (FY 1990 begins 1 April 1990).

*** U.S. and Japanese trade data does not include trade with each other.

SOURCES: OECD, *Monthly Statistics of Foreign Trade*; U.S. Dept. of Commerce *Survey of Current Business*; Japan, Ministry of Foreign Affairs, Japan's Development Assistance; Ministry of Finance; and U.S. Agency for International Development, *Congressional Presentation, FY 82 and 91* (Main Volume). Asia-Pacific region includes South/ Southwest, Southeast, East Asia, Australia/New Zealand and the Pacific Islands.

by falling equities, soft land prices, and declining profit margins, established trends suggest a continued rise in Japan's economic strength *vis-à-vis* both its Asia-Pacific neighbours and the United States at least until the next century.

The consequences of this economic power shift are difficult to foresee, especially in light of the parallel collapse of the Cold War and the apparent emergence of a more multi-polar military power balance in Asia. Not only are Japan and the United States moving towards a significant readjustment of their roles, but the roles of other major actors such as the former U.S.S.R., China and Vietnam can no longer be projected with any confidence.

Certainly the United States retains significant sources of influence in the Asia-Pacific region. Although the economic underpinnings of its power status may have weakened relative to Japan's, the United States now stands as the only true economic *and* military superpower. As demonstrated in such diverse situations as the Iraq/Kuwait crisis and the Uruguay Round of the GATT, the United States remains the single most important arbiter of the international order. International initiatives of the United States do not necessarily engender universal support, but no other country can match the power of the United States to frame issues, organize collective approaches to problems or set the agenda for multilateral negotiations. Militarily, the United States retains a strong position in the Asia-Pacific region, despite planned cutbacks in its Pacific deployments and tactical nuclear arsenal, and the impending withdrawal of U.S. forces from the Philippines.

In political terms, however, perceptions can be as important as realities. In much of the Asia-Pacific region, the traditional sources of U.S. influence tend to be seen as declining or as likely to decline in the future, while the indicators for Japan are seen as rising. Although Japan's political system is widely seen as a drag on its international role, Japan's regional influence is growing steadily as a consequence of its increasing economic weight. Meanwhile, the United States tends to be perceived — rightly or wrongly — as reducing its economic and political profile in Asia, and adopting increasingly protectionist measures to reduce its trade deficit with Asia and shore up its competitive position and economic hegemony in the Western hemisphere.

Stakes for Asia-Pacific countries

Especially in the context of the end of the Cold War and rising trade
friction between the United States and its Asian trading partners —
most notably with Japan itself — Tokyo's expanding economic role
and influence raises fundamental questions about the future structure
of Asian and Pacific economic, political and security relationships.
To what extent will Japan's economic and financial power result in
a larger political role in the Asia-Pacific region, and to what effect?
Will Japan and the United States continue to promote their national
self-interest within the overall framework of Asia-Pacific economic co-
operation and the U.S.-Japan security alliance, or will their differences
lead to an overt power rivalry? What form could such rivalry take
and what would be the prospects for the much vaunted "Asia-Pacific
century" under such conditions?

Zero-sum situation?

It remains arguable whether Japan's expanding role and influence in
the region should be viewed in zero-sum terms. After all, American
leaders, analysts and commentators have long urged that Japan assume
a greater share of the American aid and defence "burden", and the
United States and Japan share a mutual interest in stability and a
thriving global economy. Many see U.S.-Japanese interdependence so
complete that neither can seriously harm the other without hurting itself.[2] From this perspective, a positive-sum situation in which both win,
or a negative-sum situation in which both lose, may be more relevant.

In another sense, however, Japanese influence in Asia *is* increasing
at U.S. expense, with potentially significant consequences for all countries in the region. At stake are the structure and functioning of the
Asia-Pacific system, including the balance between various sources
of investment in the region, the economic "division of labour" among
countries with differing natural and human resource endowments and
varying stages of development, and the stability and security of a region
where the United States has long played the role as the most important
external balancing power.

Emerging U.S.-Japan rivalry?

While ties remain strong, there is no guarantee that the oft-proclaimed mutuality of U.S. and Japanese interests will indefinitely sustain their alliance or forestall an overt rivalry. Many already profess to see the United States and Japan as emerging economic and regional political rivals due to mutual frustration with each other's perceived nationalistic policies and a shrinking Soviet military threat. One of the more dramatic indicators is an opinion poll conducted by Louis Harris and Associates in July 1989 in which some 68 per cent of American respondents cited the economic threat from Japan as a bigger threat to the future of the United States than the Soviet military threat.³ This result was mirrored by a July 1991 *Yomiuri Shimbun* poll that showed 24 per cent rating the United States as a security threat versus 22 per cent for the Soviet Union,⁴ and another Japanese poll which showed only 48 per cent of the respondents thought that Japan had gained from its security relationship with the United States.⁵

The Persian Gulf crisis that began with Iraq's August 1990 invasion of Kuwait created new strains in U.S.-Japan relations and provoked a rethinking of the costs and benefits of the alliance on both sides. American leaders resented Japan's seemingly reluctant support of U.S. policy and Tokyo's failure to establish even a symbolic physical presence in the Gulf, despite its heavy dependence on the region's oil. For their part, the Japanese resented Washington's blunt pressure tactics and the seeming lack of appreciation of Japan's ultimate contribution of nearly US$13 billion to the allied cause.

Formal progress in resolving trade disputes through the Structural Impediments Initiative (SII), and efforts by the Japanese Government to adopt a more internationalist posture, have not yet produced much fundamental change in mutual perceptions at the level of legislative and public opinion. American congressional and press criticism of Japan's trading practices and alleged lack of commitment to international burden sharing are matched in Japan by popular books and articles that portray Americans as uncreative, arrogant, spoiled, badly governed and "racist" (towards Japan). In early 1991, the Japanese even coined a new word — *kenbei* — translated as "dislike of the United

States", in response to long-building feelings of resentment at American pressure, even as polls showed majority support for the U.S.-Japan alliance and acceptance of the need to accommodate U.S. demands for financial support in the Gulf war.[6]

Concern about a power shift in the Asia-Pacific in favour of Japan is more evident in the region itself than in the United States. Apart from a number of issue-raising but impressionistic treatments by journalists, Japan's rising influence in the region has, until very recently, received comparatively little attention.[7] According to one calculation, until his planned November 1991 trip to Tokyo to lay the ground for President George Bush's visit to Japan, Secretary of State James A. Baker III had "spent exactly one night in Tokyo during his entire time in office, a fact well known to the Japanese".[8] Some analysts judge that the United States "is in danger of ceding the region to Japan".[9] When articulated, U.S. official concern has tended to focus mainly on the perceived adverse effects on U.S. trade interests arising out of Tokyo's growing economic role in the region, rather than the potential political, foreign policy or security ramifications.

Especially in the context of the rapidly evolving situation in Europe and dramatic shifts in East-West relations, both U.S. and Japanese policies in Asia have appeared more reactive than creative. American leaders thus far have appeared to lack a clear vision for the future role of the United States in the region, apart from maintaining some form of the status quo, or a conceptual framework for adjusting to Japan's growing economic power and influence. Japanese leaders say that Japan must accept "greater responsibility" for the future growth and stability of the Asia-Pacific region but to date have tended to shy away from actions that would subordinate their country's economic and commercial interests to a broader concept of enlightened national self-interest.

Although the 1991 disintegration of central authority in the Soviet Union has revalidated the position of the United States as the pre-eminent global military power, the practical effects in Asia and the Pacific may not parallel the global situation. The very asymmetry of U.S. and Japanese sources of power — military and economic — gives rise to concerns about their future roles in a region where the interrelationship between these dimensions of power is elusive but unquestionably important.

How much most Asia-Pacific countries themselves have thought through the ramifications of Japan's rising power and influence is questionable. Some leaders, such as Singapore's former Prime Minister Lee Kuan Yew, have called attention to the need to maintain a balanced power structure in the region and have actively sought to generate continued interest and involvement on the part of the United States, Canada and the European Community (EC) nations. Others, notably Malaysia's Prime Minister Dr Mahathir bin Mohamad, have floated proposals that appear aimed at strengthening Japan's hand *vis-à-vis* the United States in a bid for greater Asian solidarity. In general, many Asia-Pacific leaders appear less concerned about the long term implications of the new patterns of investment, aid, trade and political relationships than in maintaining the current momentum of national economic growth.

The following analysis seeks to provide a framework for considering the ramifications of Japan's expanding economic role and influence in the Asia-Pacific region, and the policy implications for the main actors, most notably the market economies with the biggest stake and an established record of co-operation — the United States, Japan, the Asian Newly Industrializing Economies (NIEs), the Association of South East Asian Nations (ASEAN), Australia, and New Zealand. The following chapters document Japan's emergence as the regional "core economy"; review the factors that may influence Tokyo's future political and military role; assess the problems and prospects for Japanese leadership in Asia; pose alternative scenarios for the evolving Asia-Pacific economic, political and security order; analyse the factors and conditions that may determine which, if any, of those alternative scenarios might prevail; and consider the policy implications for Asia-Pacific countries.

2
Evolution of the Asia-Pacific economic order during the 1980s

The decade of the 1980s saw a quantum increase in the size of the Asia-Pacific economies and the growth of intra-regional trade. Intra-Asian trade is growing rapidly in response to new patterns of offshore investment by Japan and the NIEs and the resultant growth of export-oriented manufacturing and incomes. With Japan and the NIEs accounting for 69 per cent of the total, intra-Asian exports totalled US$270 billion in 1989, compared with Asian exports of US$206 million to North America and US$182 billion to Europe. Led by manufactured goods, intra-Asian exports grew at nearly 30 per cent per year during the period 1986–88, then slipped to 12.1 per cent growth in 1989. Trade among the NIEs alone totalled US$28 billion in 1989, up 17 per cent over 1988.[10] Intra-ASEAN trade totalled US$50 billion in 1990, a five-fold increase over the level of the mid-1970s.[11]

Japan, the United States, and the Asian countries themselves have all played important roles in bringing about this rapid growth of intra-Asian and trans-Pacific economic ties. Although Japan has emerged as the main catalyst of regional integration, the role of the U.S. economy as a seemingly insatiable consumer of Asian manufactured goods has given the region its main export dynamism.[12] Both the NIEs and the ASEAN countries have played their parts through economic reforms emphasizing free markets, privatization of state-owned enterprises, export-led growth and favourable terms for foreign investment.

Significantly different interpretations can be given to these changes in the structure of regional economic ties. One perspective emphasizes that "both the United States and Japan have come to dominate the trade of these [Asia-Pacific] nations to a greater degree than in the past."[13] Another view stresses the asymmetry of the U.S. and Japanese roles, especially the large U.S. trade deficit, on the one hand, and the large Japanese surplus, on the other. From the second perspective, the presumed unsustainability of the U.S. trade deficit looms as a more important factor than the recent role of the U.S. economy as an engine of growth for the region. A third, more recent perspective, is that the Asia-Pacific region, with Japan as its economic nerve centre, has acquired the critical mass necessary for a large measure of self-sustaining growth as part of a loosely defined "Yen Bloc".

Japan's Emergence as the "core economy" of the Asia-Pacific region

Although Japan's role as an exporter of manufactured goods and an importer of primary products from Asia-Pacific countries is long-standing, its post-1985 emergence as the leading source of capital and technology, and as a growing market for manufactured goods, has made Japan the "core economy" of the region. Private Japanese business investment is fuelling rapid growth in the NIEs and would-be NIEs such as Thailand and Malaysia, while bilateral economic assistance underpins the weaker economies in Asia and the Pacific Islands.

Japan's current role derives primarily from the huge trade surpluses built up during the 1980s and the near doubling of the value of the yen against the U.S. dollar following the Plaza Accord of September 1985.[14] The currency revaluation made Japanese manufactured goods more expensive, but also effectively doubled the dollar value of Japan's aid budget and the investment buying power of the yen. In effect, Japan recycled a substantial proportion of its surplus U.S. dollars to its Asia-Pacific neighbours in the form of increased aid and new business investment. As new offshore production facilities have come on line as a result of this recycling of Japan's trade surplus earnings, part of the trade surplus itself is being transferred to other countries' accounts in the form of increased exports of Japanese-brand manufactured goods to the United States and other third markets. By one estimate, "when the flow of goods from Japan to the United States through third countries in East Asia is traced, it shows that about 70 per cent of Japan's trade surplus is American in origin".[15]

Manufacturing and market-penetration focus of Japan's investment in the Asia-Pacific region

New Japanese investment in the Asia-Pacific region totalled US$11.2 billion in Japanese fiscal year 1990 (Table 2.1), nearly six times more than the 1985 figure and nearly twice the investment of U.S. companies during approximately the same period (calendar 1990). The disparity was even greater in the FY 1986–89 time frame. During FY 1990, for the first time in recent years, Japanese direct investment declined abruptly in Asia and all other regions, as the fall in stock prices and levelling-off of land prices forced banks and businesses to cover domestic capital requirements. Significantly, most of this decline occurred in financial and real estate investment, not in manufacturing investment. American investment, meanwhile, jumped abruptly by US$3 billion in Australia-New Zealand and another US$3.5 billion in Asia (half of which was accounted by Singapore alone), closing slightly what had been a rapidly widening investment gap.

Investment in East and Southeast Asia occupies a special place in Japan's global economic reach, and its relative position seems unlikely to decline markedly in the next few years. On a world-wide basis, the cumulative US$47.5 billion invested by Japanese companies in Asia in 1990 lagged behind holdings in North America (mainly the United States) and Europe, and accounted for only about 15 per cent of Japan's global investment. However, the proportion of investment going into *manufacturing* in Asia in recent years has been considerably higher than for other regions. As of 1989, manufacturing absorbed 38.4 per cent of aggregate Japanese investment in Asia versus only 18.4 per cent in the case of Japanese investment in the United States and only about

Table 2.1

Japanese direct investment in Asia and Oceania, FY 1985–90

	FY 85	FY 86	FY 87	FY 88	FY 89	FY 90	FY 51–90	U.S. Reference Total Year End 1990 (Historical Cost Basis)
NIEs	718	1,531	2,580	3,264	4,900	3,355	23,274	14,877
Hong Kong	131	502	1,072	1,662	1,898	1,785	9,850	6,537
South Korea	134	436	647	483	606	284	4,138	2,096
Singapore	339	302	494	747	1,902	840	6,555	3,971
Taiwan	114	291	367	372	494	446	2,731	2,273
ASEAN	597	554	1,030	1,966	2,782	3,242	20,882	8,400
Brunei	1	1	1	—	—	—	109	−22
Indonesia	408	250	545	586	631	1,105	11,540	3,827
Malaysia	79	158	163	387	673	725	3,231	1,425
Philippines	61	21	72	134	202	258	1,580	1,655
Thailand	48	124	250	859	1,276	1,154	4,422	1,515
China (PRC)	100	226	1,226	296	438	349	2,823	289
Other Asia	20	16	32	43	118	108	540	910
Total Asia	1,435	2,327	4,868	5,569	8,238	7,054	47,519	24,476

Table 2.1 (Continued)

	FY 85	FY 86	FY 87	FY 88	FY 89	FY 90	FY 51–90	U.S. Reference Total Year End 1990 (Historical Cost Basis)
Oceania	525	992	1,413	2,669	4,618	4,166	18,098	17,911
Australia	468	881	1,222	2,413	4,256	3,669	16,063	14,529
New Zealand	23	93	21	117	101	231	925	3,139
Pacific Islands	34	18	70	139	261	266	1,110	243
Total Asia-Pacific	1,960	3,319	6,281	8,238	12,856	11,220	65,617	42,387

SOURCES: Japanese Ministry of Financial Statistics, U.S. Department of Commerce, *Survey of Current Business* (August 1991).

17.7 per cent in the case of Europe (Figure 2.1). Investment in the electrical machinery (electronics) industry accounted for the single largest share of Japanese manufacturing investment in Asia in recent years (Figure 2.2).

In addition to the post-1985 rise in the yen, Japanese domestic cost factors such as a growing labour shortage, rising land prices and increasingly stringent pollution control measures have also played an important role in fuelling offshore investment. A February 1990 report by the Japan Development Bank noted that, of various reasons cited by Japanese companies for establishing offshore manufacturing facilities in Asia in 1987, some 54.7 per cent of the respondents cited the goal of reducing labour costs.[16]

For investment by small and medium-sized Japanese companies — the ones hardest hit by rising costs — Asia is far and away the most important manufacturing investment destination. Such relocation has been actively abetted by the powerful Ministry of International Trade and Industry (MITI) and its Japan External Trade Organization (JETRO), both to help these companies remain competitive or survive economic restructuring at home and to provide an offshore supplier base for larger Japanese companies. The proportion of offshore manufacturing investment in Asia by small and medium-sized firms grew from 57.9 per cent of the world-wide total for such firms in 1984, to 72.7 per cent in 1987, then dropped back to 65.6 per cent in 1988.[17]

The ripple effect of rapidly growing Japanese offshore investment is changing the economic face of the Asia-Pacific region. The physical landscape of Asian cities and their environs is coming to be dominated by Japanese business offices, hotels and manufacturing plants. Increasing numbers of consumer products bearing brand names such as Sony, Panasonic and Canon are being produced in Japanese-owned factories in Asia, rather than in Japan itself. Japanese tourists, business travellers, and expatriate employees have become mainstays of regional airlines, hotels, and related service industries in much of the Asia-Pacific region, with spillover impact on emerging indigenous middle class lifestyles. Karaoke lounges and Japanese pop singers now compete with Western popular culture symbols in burgeoning Asian capitals.

Even more important is the impetus to regional integration resulting

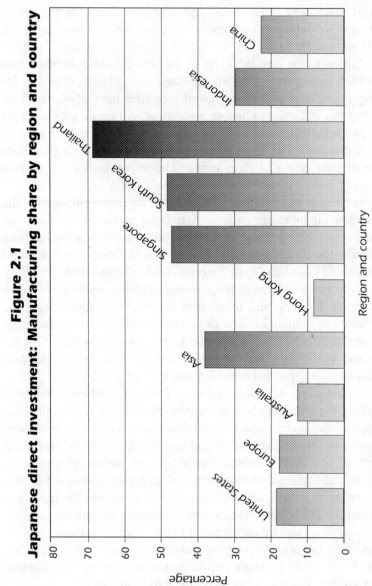

Figure 2.1
Japanese direct investment: Manufacturing share by region and country

NOTE: Basis is total FDI as of end FY 1990.
SOURCE: Ministry of Finance.

Figure 2.2
Japan's Investment in Asia: Annual new investment categorized by major types, FY 1985–89

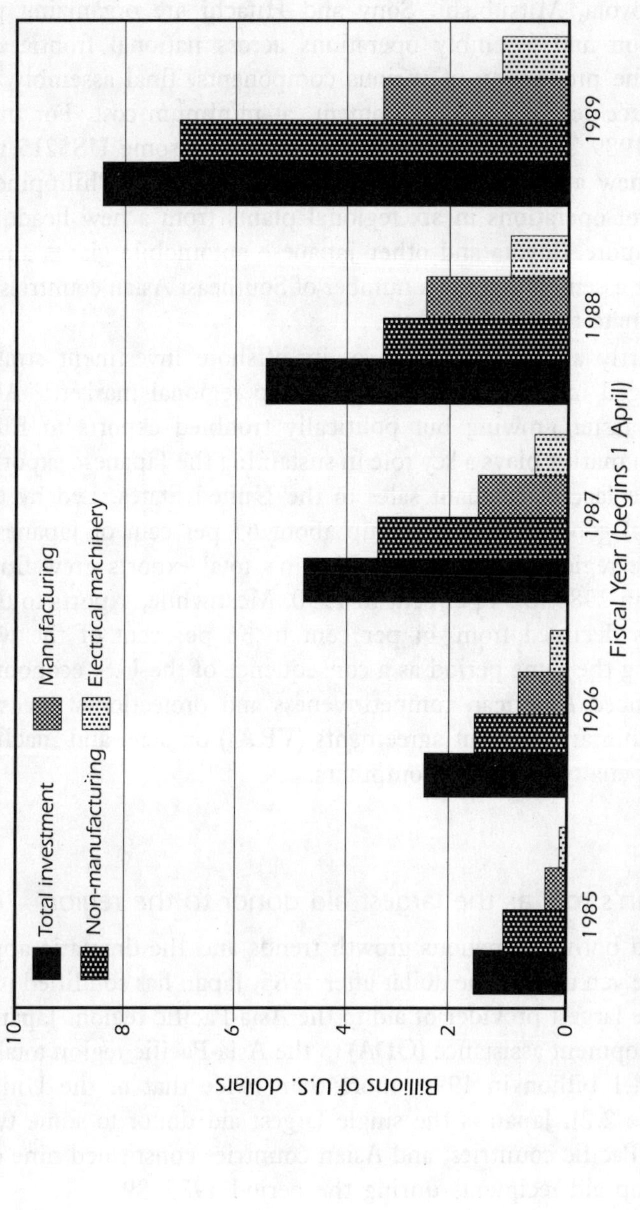
Total investment
Non-manufacturing
Manufacturing
Electrical machinery
Billions of U.S. dollars
0
2
4
6
8
10
1985
1986
1987
1988
1989
Fiscal Year (begins 1 April)

SOURCE: Ministry of Finance.

from Japanese offshore manufacturing operations. Companies such as Toyota, Mitsubishi, Sony and Hitachi are organizing parts production and assembly operations across national frontiers to carry out the production of various components, final assembly, and even product design and development, at minimum cost. For instance, in late 1989 Tokyo announced plans to invest some US$215 million in two new automobile plants in Malaysia and the Philippines, and to control operations in six regional plants from a new headquarters in Singapore. Toyota and other Japanese automobile giants already have major assembly lines in a number of Southeast Asian countries, and they dominate the local markets.

Partly as a consequence of its offshore investment strategy, Asia emerged in early 1991 as Japan's top regional market.[18] Along with even faster growing but politically troubled exports to Europe, the Asian market plays a key role in sustaining the Japanese export machine in the face of stagnant sales to the United States. Led by exports of capital goods, which make up about 65 per cent of Japanese exports to the region, Asia's share of Japan's total exports grew from 28 per cent in 1985 to 34 per cent in 1990. Meanwhile, exports to the United States declined from 44 per cent to 36 per cent of the world total during the same period as a consequence of the U.S. economic slump, enhanced American competitiveness and protectionist measures such as voluntary restraint agreements (VRAs) on steel and machine tools, and penalty tariffs on computers.

Japan's role as the largest aid donor to the region

Based both on previous growth trends and the dramatic appreciation of the yen against the dollar after 1985, Japan has solidified its position as the largest provider of aid to the Asia-Pacific region. Japan's official development assistance (ODA) to the Asia-Pacific region totalled about US$4.1 billion in 1990, more than twice that of the United States (Table 2.2). Japan is the single largest aid donor to some twenty-five Asia-Pacific countries, and Asian countries constituted nine of Japan's ten top aid recipients during the period 1985–89.

Table 2.2
Geographical distribution of Japan's bilateral ODA
(Net disbursements, in millions of US$)

	1980		1988		1989		1990	
Asia	1,383	(70.5)	4,039	(62.8)	4,240	(62.5)	4,117	(59.3)
Northeast Asia	82	(4.2)	730	(11.4)	919	(13.2)	835	(12.0)
Southeast Asia	861	(44.0)	2,197	(34.2)	2,226	(32.8)	2,379	(34.3)
ASEAN	703	(35.9)	1,920	(29.9)	2,132	(31.5)	2,299	(33.1)
Southwest Asia	435	(22.2)	1,109	(17.3)	1,091	(16.1)	898	(12.9)
Unspecified	5	(0.3)	3	(0.1)	4	(0.0)	4	(0.0)
Middle East	204	(10.4)	583	(9.1)	368	(5.4)	705	(10.2)
Africa	223	(11.4)	884	(13.8)	1,040	(15.3)	792	(11.4)
Central and South America	118	(6.0)	399	(6.2)	563	(8.3)	561	(8.1)
Oceania	12	(0.6)	93	(1.4)	98	(1.4)	114	(1.6)
Europe	−1.5	(—)	4	(0.1)	11	(0.2)	158	(2.3)
Unallocable	1	(1.2)	425	(6.6)	458	(6.8)	494	(7.1)
Total Bilateral ODA	1,961	(100.0)	6,426	(100.0)	6,779	(100.0)	6,940	(100.0)

SOURCE: Ministry of Foreign Affairs, *Japan's Official Development Assistance, 1988 and 1990 Annual Reports*. (Supplemented by preliminary 1990 data from the Japanese version of the 1991 report.)

Unlike the United States, which has been "graduating" Asian developing countries from its development assistance programme, Japan views aid as "economic co-operation" and traditionally has channelled about two-thirds of its overall aid to Asia-Pacific countries, half of that to *relatively* well off Southeast Asian countries.[19] (The ratio dropped to 59.3 per cent for FY 1990 as a result of extraordinary Japanese contributions to affected states in the Persian Gulf war.[20]) In marked contrast to U.S. aid programmes, loans for infrastructure development projects — lucrative sources of business for Japanese engineering, construction and trading companies — are the predominant form of Japanese aid.

The rapid growth of Tokyo's bilateral ODA, contributions to multilateral lending institutions, and soft export credits has caused the poorer countries of Asia to look increasingly to Japan to help finance their budget and trade deficits and alleviate their problems of lagging development and unemployment. According to one expert on Japan's aid programme, "Japan's aid equals 15% to 20% of the budget expenditures of virtually every Asian country", a factor that in his view "inevitably means an expansion of Japanese power and influence".[21]

Continued economic importance of the United States

During the 1980s, the U.S. market served as an important engine of growth for the Asia-Pacific economies, and it remains a key factor in the region's prosperity. By one calculation, between 1980 and 1984 the United States absorbed an estimated 71 per cent of the growth in manufactured exports from East and Southeast Asia and the Pacific, while Japan took only 9 per cent.[22] During the period 1985–90, the United States took slightly over US$1 trillion in goods from the region, including Japan, and ran a cumulative trade *deficit* of US$499 billion, while Japan ran large trade surpluses with most of the same countries. As recently as 1989, the U.S. market absorbed 27.1 per cent of the exports of the ASEAN countries and the NIEs, while Japan absorbed only 15.3 per cent.[23]

The role of the U.S. market in the economic dynamism of the region would be difficult to overestimate. Not only did exports to the United States contribute directly to rapid growth in NIEs and developing countries of the region, but the huge trade surpluses earned by Japan were also partially recycled to other regional countries (and elsewhere) in the form of Japanese investment, aid and purchases of goods. The U.S. market assumes even greater importance as a consequence of Japan's own strong export position and its low propensity to import. The highly asymmetrical trade relationships of the United States and Japan with the Asia-Pacific region are shown graphically, in Figures 2.3 and 2.4.

American business investment remains very important to a number of Asia-Pacific countries, especially Taiwan, Hong Kong, Singapore, the Philippines and Australia. A comparison of U.S. and Japanese direct investment in the region, which some argue is methodologically unsound,[24] shows Japan with US$65.6 billion in investment approved by host governments and notified to the Japanese Ministry of Finance as of 31 March 1990 (FY 1990), versus a US$43.3 billion equity position for U.S. firms as of the end of calendar 1990. In Asia, the ratio is roughly 2:1 in Japan's favour.

Total U.S. investment in the Asia-Pacific region may still compare roughly to that of Japan if calculated on the same basis since, in crude terms, Japanese data measures *intent* to invest while U.S. figures reflect actual capital flows (Appendix A). The historical cost basis of both sets of data also tends to exaggerate Japan's advantage, since most of its investment is newer. These issues aside, American investment remains highly valued since U.S.-owned multinationals generally tend to transfer more technology than Japanese companies and use substantially higher proportions of local personnel as managers and technicians. American investment also tends to generate proportionately much higher levels of exports to the U.S. market than Japanese investment in regard to the Japanese market.

The United States also plays an important and often under-recognized role in human resources development in the region. It remains a significant aid donor to the lowest income countries of South Asia, in the Philippines and in some of the Pacific Islands, and is a leading contributor to multilateral lending agencies. Unlike Japan, whose aid

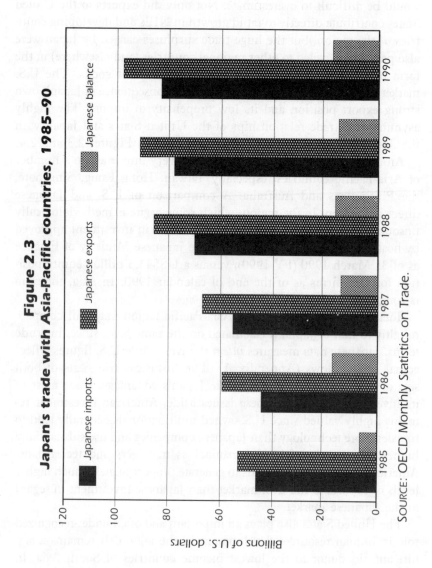

Figure 2.3
Japan's trade with Asia-Pacific countries, 1985–90

Japanese imports   Japanese exports   Japanese balance

Billions of U.S. dollars

1985 1986 1987 1988 1989 1990

SOURCE: OECD Monthly Statistics on Trade.

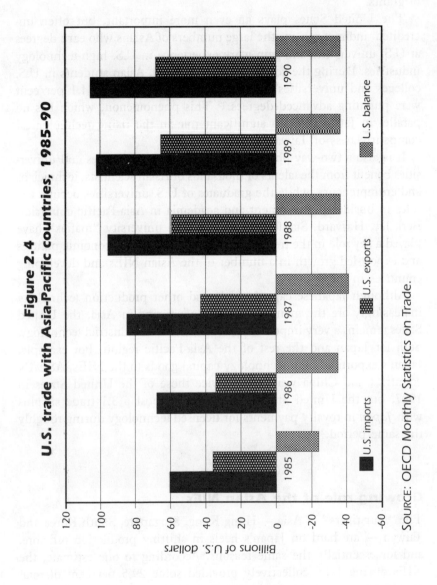

Figure 2.4
U.S. trade with Asia-Pacific countries, 1985–90

SOURCE: OECD Monthly Statistics on Trade.

normally takes the form of soft loans, most U.S. aid is in the form
of grants.

The United States plays an even more important, but often un-
credited, indirect role via the large numbers of Asians who earn degrees
at U.S. universities and gain work experience in U.S. high-technology
industries. During the academic year 1989–90, Asian students in U.S.
colleges and universities numbered 208,110, of whom 54.1 per cent
were pursuing advanced degrees.[25] This phenomenon, which has no
parallel in Japan, plays a significant role in the rising technological
competitiveness of Taiwan and South Korea.

It is also a two-way phenomenon. American companies and universities benefit from the talents of thousands of Asian scientists, technicians
and entrepreneurs, while the graduates of U.S. universities occupy key
roles in business, government and academia in Asia-Pacific countries.
Berkeley, Harvard, Stanford and other élite university "mafias" have
played a key role in the trend towards market-oriented economic policies
and export-led growth in a number of the Asian NIEs and developing
countries in the region.

Although Japanese capital goods and other production technology
increasingly are the mainstays of manufacturing in Asia, the United
States remains a very important source of licensed industrial technology,
both for Japan and the rest of the Asia-Pacific region. For example,
Japan's exports of high technology capital goods to the NIEs, ASEAN
countries and China were about twice those of the United States in
1987, but the United States still enjoyed almost a 3:1 trade surplus
with *Japan* in royalty payments for licensed technology during roughly
the same period.[26]

Growing role of the Asian NIEs

The "four tigers" of Asia — Hong Kong, Singapore, South Korea and
Taiwan — are hard on Japan's heels in shifting production offshore,
and for essentially the same reasons. According to one estimate, the
NIEs during 1988 collectively provided some 29.5 per cent of total
manufacturing investment in four ASEAN countries — Thailand,

Malaysia, Indonesia and the Philippines — compared to 30 per cent for Japan.[27] Increasingly, companies based in the NIEs are also competing effectively with Japanese multinationals for engineering and construction business in the Asia-Pacific region.

Initially, the rush of South Korea and Taiwan to invest in lower wage areas of Asia stemmed both from their large trade surpluses and from successful pressure on them by the United States in the 1987–88 time period to revalue their currencies upward against the dollar. At present, however, all of the NIEs are experiencing rising domestic costs and inflationary pressures that threaten to undercut earlier gains made against Japanese companies in the lower and middle technology ends of the global consumer goods market.

Taiwan recently became the second leading source of new investment in the Philippines, and it has become an important investor in Hong Kong, which serves as an intermediary for officially impermissible direct investment in the Peoples' Republic of China (PRC). In 1989, Taiwan was the second-ranking source of foreign investment funds in Malaysia and Thailand. According to one calculation, Taiwanese companies invested some US$2.1 billion in Malaysia in that year alone, versus US$2.9 billion for Japan.[28]

South Korea also plays an increasingly important role in offshore investment in Asia. Its international competitiveness is under strain due to a similarly strong appreciation of the South Korean won against the dollar in recent years, and rising labour strife. Long a model of export-led growth, South Korea's export surplus shrunk markedly in 1989 and the current account balance turned negative in 1990. As a consequence of decreasing comparative advantage at home, particularly in textiles, South Korean firms are becoming important investors in Indonesia and the Philippines.

Singapore and Hong Kong have been more affected by rising labour costs and shortages of skilled workers than currency appreciation. Labour-short Singapore is providing substantial investment in Malaysia, Indonesia and other ASEAN countries in hope of moving up-market as a financial, technological and high-quality services centre. As a result, Singapore has emerged as the number three investor in Malaysia (US$911 million in 1989), after Japan and Taiwan.[29]

Hong Kong has long been the dominant investor in China's coastal Guandong province, where low-cost suppliers have been the key to keeping its exports competitive in world markets. Spurred by concerns about the impending takeover by China in 1997, Hong Kong money is now pushing into Southeast Asia. Hong Kong stood second in cumulative investment in Indonesia for the period 1967–89, well below Japan but ahead of the United States.[30]

The increasing economic role of the NIEs as offshore investors in other Asia-Pacific countries still appears to have considerably less overall significance than that of Japan. Although some have launched small aid programmes, the NIEs cannot match the synergistic impact of Japan's combined investment, aid and trade roles, nor its international political influence. None the less, the rising role of the NIEs can be viewed as a bell-wether of a deepening diversification of the political economy of the Asia-Pacific region, even as Japan's prominence increases.

The overseas Chinese connection

In addition to national economic entities, the 40 million or so overseas Chinese in East and Southeast Asia have also played a significant role in the evolution of the political economy of the Asia-Pacific region, sometimes in their capacity as local traders, sometimes as joint partners of Japanese and other foreign investors, and sometimes as foreign investors themselves. Apart from being the indigenous majority in Hong Kong, Taiwan and Singapore, ethnic Chinese largely control the organized sectors of a number of Southeast Asian countries where they are distinct minorities. According to one estimate, resident Chinese control about three-fourths of private domestic capital in Indonesia, 68 per cent in the Philippines and 60 per cent in Thailand, even though they number less than three per cent of the Indonesian population, around one per cent in the Philippines and less than ten per cent Thailand.[31] The Chinese also own the bulk of private domestic capital in Malaysia, where their significant 37 per cent share of the total population creates added sources of domestic political tension.

The Chinese "connection" undergirds much of the growth of intra-Asian investment and trade, and increasingly it serves as a key link between Asia and North America, notably in the case of Hong Kong immigrants in Vancouver and other Canadian and U.S. cities. In many cases, the actual origins of Chinese investment funds are uncertain due to the global nature of Chinese family and business connections. According to some reports, a portion of the Taiwanese investment in Malaysia is actually local Chinese money that is "laundered" through Taiwan to circumvent regulations that favour foreign over domestic investment.

Traditionally, Chinese entrepreneurs have concentrated on trade and commerce, and have seldom engaged in manufacturing except as licensees of multinationals or in government-protected monopolies.[32] In the past decade, however, the combination of economic liberalization in the ASEAN countries and the inflow of Japanese investment has drawn Chinese capital more and more into the realm of manufacturing.[33]

The existing predominance of Chinese capital in Southeast Asian economies makes Chinese-owned business houses the logical partners of Japanese firms, not to mention ethnic Chinese investors from Hong Kong, Taiwan and Singapore. For example, the PT Astra International group in Indonesia, a Chinese-controlled conglomerate, makes motorcycles in a joint venture with Honda, trucks and small cars with Toyota and Daihatsu, construction equipment with Komatsu, and diesel trucks with Nissan.[34] Numerous other examples can also be cited in Malaysia, Thailand and Indonesia.

The relative openness of Southeast Asian countries to foreign investment appears largely to be a function of the degree of influence exercised over economic policy by the Chinese business class. Thailand and the Philippines are the most open, while Malaysia seeks to manipulate the balance of resident Chinese and foreign capital with an objective of promoting the development of an ethnic Malay entrepreneurial class. Indonesia, where the tiny Chinese minority is economically vital but politically suppressed, has been slower to liberalize its foreign investment policy. Since the early 1980s, however, a period coinciding with the softening of oil prices, Jakarta has steadily liberalized terms for foreign investment. Apart from positive motives aimed at increasing the efficiency of the economy, the Indonesian Government requires

foreign investment to generate enough exports to service its heavy
foreign debt. The Soeharto government has increasingly moved towards
open acknowledgment of the importance of both Chinese-owned "con-
glomerates" and foreign investment in Indonesia's economic development.

3
Structural patterns in Japan's economic role in Asia

The complexity of Japan's interaction with its Asia-Pacific neighbours defies easy categorization and analysis, but understanding the inter-relationships is crucial to assessing the broader implications of Japan's growing role. This chapter first examines Japan's overall regional economic strategy and its interaction with individual countries or sub-regions. Then it considers the overall systemic and functional linkages in order to better appreciate the profound impact of Japan's rapidly rising aid and investment on the wider political economy of the Asia-Pacific region.

"Flying geese" and the new division of labour

Flush with growing self-confidence, a number of Japanese academics, bureaucrats and political leaders have openly articulated new concepts for the organization of production and trade in Asia. These notions are based on implicit acceptance of the superiority of Japan's pro-duction system and the explicit desire to integrate those countries of the Asia-Pacific region that have favourable economic policy and labour conditions into a greater Japanese economy. Over the longer term, Japanese economic managers appear to seek a "division of labour" that maximizes each country's comparative advantage, thus fostering complementary rather than competitive patterns of industrialization.[35]

One notion, popularized a decade ago by Dr Saburo Okita, foreign minister under the Ohira government in the late 1970s, is the concept of the Asian countries as part of a formation of flying geese.[36] Japan, with its larger economy and higher technological level, is in the lead position. Ranged behind it in order of their economic strength and levels of technological sophistication are the NIEs, the ASEAN countries and, finally, the lower income countries of South Asia and Indochina. As seen by Okita, the successive waves of "geese" will gain from the experience of the leaders and tend to close the technological gap, leading to the eventual horizontal integration of the Asia-Pacific region. This outcome is viewed as a direct result of the pro-investment, market-oriented, export-led growth policies followed by the most economically dynamic Asian countries.[37]

A related Japanese concept is that there is a natural division of labour in Asia that conforms to each country's "revealed" comparative advantage — i.e. demonstrated by its trade performance. In analysing the growing success of the NIEs in penetrating the Japanese market, Japanese economists have seen the gains mainly from labour cost advantages, although in the future the NIEs' higher-technology exports to Japan are expected to expand as their own investment in research and development and supporting industries grows.[38]

Bilateral and sub-regional relationships

The "flying geese" model finds inspiration in the diverse levels of economic development and resource endowments in the Asia-Pacific region. At present, the forms of Japan's interaction with the region can be categorized loosely into three types. With the dynamic Asian NIEs, the first wave of "geese" behind the leader, Japan's economic interaction follows a complementary-competitive pattern having attributes both of interdependence and rivalry. Japan's ties with the developing parts of Asia, including China, tend to be dominated by economic co-operation relationships that are highly complementary, albeit skewed in Japan's favour. Japan's involvement with Australia and New Zealand is somewhat more complex and multi-faceted due to the advanced nature of their economic and political development, but generally follows a complementary rather than a competitive pattern.

Newly Industrializing Economies

Although the so-called "four tigers" of Asia initially constituted the first targets of large-scale Japanese investment, their relatively advanced state of development has increasingly made them competitors across a wide range of medium-to-high technology industries. The NIEs continue to occupy an important place in Japan's global and regional economic reach as suppliers of chemicals, steel and other inputs for its industries, as sources of lower-end consumer goods, and as major absorbers of Japanese capital goods and components. Their development pattern has been shaped by high trade surpluses with the United States, their main market, and high trade deficits with Japan.

Annual new Japanese investment in the NIEs grew from US$718 million in Japanese FY 1985 to US$4.9 billion in FY 1989, then dipped back to US$3.4 billion in FY 1990. The cumulative value of its approvals and notifications of investment in the four NIEs totalled US$23.3 billion at the end of FY 1990, nominally about twice that of the United States. Until about 1990, Japan had displaced the United States as the single largest source of new investment in the NIEs.[39] Japan's investment is highest in Hong Kong, which received nearly half of Japanese investment in the NIEs in recent years, followed by Singapore, South Korea and Taiwan.

While the NIEs collectively remain the largest recipients of Japanese investment, rising costs have led to a *relative* shift of investment, as measured in rate of growth, to the ASEAN countries. Most of this shift has been accounted for by South Korea and Taiwan, where new Japanese investment has been relatively flat in the past few years. Recently, due to rising discrimination against Japanese products by Korea, significant labour unrest and quality control problems, Japanese firms appear to have developed an active aversion to new investment there.

Individually, the NIEs show as many differences as similarities, the main common denominator being their middle income status, "Confucianist" cultural heritage, and related factors such as nearly universal literacy. In their relationships with Japan, Hong Kong and Singapore serve primarily as production bases for exports to third countries, especially the United States. Both run very large trade deficits with Japan. Although Singapore's exports to Japan have been growing faster than its imports, it still ran a US$7.2 billion trade deficit with Japan in 1990, with imports three times its exports. Because of the more broadly based nature of their economies, Taiwan and South Korea, on the other hand, engage in a more extensive two-way trade with Japan. Ironically, due to a greater sense of rivalry with Japan, the imbalances are felt more keenly and have tended to sour relations with Tokyo.

By mid-1991 Japan's mounting trade surpluses with South Korea and Taiwan had become a major source of concern on the part of all three countries. As of the first half of 1991, Japan's overall trade surplus with South Korea soared to US$4.1 billion as against US$5.75 billion for all of 1990. Japan's surplus with Taiwan rose to US$3.82 billion in the first half of 1991, versus US$6.93 billion for all of 1990.[40] In absolute terms, Hong Kong and Singapore experienced even larger deficits with Japan, but the character of these economies as trade entrepôts and offshore production bases for exports to third markets has made the imbalances less politically sensitive.

The rapid growth of South Korean and Taiwanese exports to Japan in the 1985–88 period appeared to many analysts to reflect a fundamental shift of comparative advantage in certain medium-level technologies, especially in sectors such as steel, chemicals, and some consumer electronics products, and related restructuring of the Japanese economy. The abrupt levelling off of import growth beginning in 1989 appears to have multiple causes, including currency revaluations, rising domestic costs, a shift of Japanese investment towards Southeast Asia, and market resistance in Japan to NIEs goods, especially relatively poor quality Korean manufactures.

The problems of NIEs exporters reflect an undercurrent of technological rivalry between them and Japan. Once Japanese companies decide to move lower technology production offshore or abandon a product line all together, as in the case of black and white televisions, the Japanese market opens up. But in higher technology, higher value added areas, Japanese companies, abetted by MITI, fight tenaciously to maintain their lead. South Korea and Taiwan in particular have been struggling hard to eliminate their technological dependence on Japan by creating an indigenous capacity to build vital components such as computer memory chips. But they face an uphill battle as a result of less well educated labour forces, Japan's vastly larger research and development investment levels and larger domestic market base.

ASEAN and Southeast Asia

Japan's economic involvement in Southeast Asia is long-standing, but it has broadened and deepened rapidly since the mid-1980s. At present, Japan's growing economic involvement in Southeast Asia is focused in the ASEAN countries, although Japan is also the prime trading partner and aid-giver to Burma and is poised to take the lead in the development of the countries of Indochina once underlying political issues are resolved.

Aid to Southeast Asian countries, primarily loans for infrastructure development, totalled US$2.2 billion in 1989, and accounted for about one-third of total bilateral and multilateral Japanese aid disbursements (Table 3.1). This compared to about US$440 million in economic *and* military aid to Southeast Asia by the United States during approximately the same period (FY 1990), of which US$350 million went to the Philippines alone.

Japan has emerged as the number one new investor in the six ASEAN countries, with cumulative investment as of March 1990 of about US$27.4 billion (Table 3.1). Japan's share of total foreign investment in ASEAN countries ranges from about 25 per cent in Indonesia to more than half in Thailand, based on estimates from national investment boards. Other informal estimates circulating in Southeast Asia credit the Japanese with even larger shares, and with unique privileges such as the right to employ proportionately more

Table 3.1
Japan's bilateral ODA to
Southeast Asian countries, FY 1990
(In US$ millions)

Country	Loan Aid	Grants Grant Aid	Grants Technical Co-operation	Total	% of Total Bilateral Aid Received (1988)
ASEAN					
Brunei	—	—	3.1	3.1	87.7
Indonesia	700.7	58.3	108.7	867.7	65.8
Malaysia	312.3	1.8	58.5	372.6	25.7
Philippines	494.3	91.1	62.0	647.5	67.7
Singapore	−24.8	—	14.3	−10.4	54.3
Thailand	246.2	76.0	96.3	418.6	70.2
Other SEA					
Myanmar	28.0	30.2	3.1	61.3	78.0
Cambodia	—	—	0.2	0.2	8.8
Laos	−1.8	15.5	3.6	17.3	19.4
Vietnam	—	—	1.3	1.3	2.4

SOURCE: Ministry of Foreign Affairs, *Japan's Official Development Assistance, 1990 and 1991 Annual Reports.* (Japanese version.)

of their nationals at all levels of their business operations and even in the households of Japanese expatriates. The tens of thousands of overseas Japanese in Southeast Asian capitals and manufacturing zones are a distinctly visible and sometimes troubling presence.

Singapore's pivotal geographic location, favourable investment climate, efficient infrastructure, pro-active strategy of restructuring its economy and upgrading its work force have been successful in bolstering the island republic's role as a high-technology manufacturing centre and a regional headquarters for Japanese and other foreign investors. At the same time, Singapore itself is developing an economic hinterland via investment in the Malaysian state of Johor and nearby Batam Island in Indonesia's Riau Archipelago, under the rubric of the "Triangle of Growth", that may become an additional platform for Japanese investment and export growth. Hong Kong enjoys similar advantages due to the rapid growth of neighbouring Guandong Province and adjacent areas of coastal China.

As the single largest net exporter of capital and technology and largest consumer of their traditional products, Japan has fashioned a generally complementary relationship between itself and the Southeast Asian developing countries, albeit one skewed in Tokyo's favour. As can be seen in Table 3.2, Japan's traditional trade deficit with the Southeast Asian region gave way to a growing trade surplus beginning in 1989. Preliminary trade figures show a continuation of this trend in 1991. Two-way trade in recent years has been distinguished by fast growing exports of Japanese capital goods, components and consumer products; high but relatively stagnant (in dollar volume) imports of raw materials and tropical products; and rising but still comparatively low imports of manufactured goods and semi-finished manufactures from Japanese-owned plants.

Collectively the ASEAN states now rank third after the United States and the EC as Japan's largest trading partner, but trade is sharply balanced in Japan's favour. Japanese exports to the four ASEAN developing countries grew by 194 per cent during the period 1986–90 versus 74.2 per cent growth in imports by Japan from those same countries (Appendix B).

China

Japan maintains a complex and delicate relationship with China, its most important neighbour after the Russian Republic, and has had a strong interest in China's economic and political modernization, and its emergence as a participant in the world economy. Apart from the importance of its physical size and military potential, China possesses important oil and coal reserves, strategic minerals, and provides a huge potential market for Japanese goods. China presently enjoys a substantial trade surplus with Japan, which imported US$12 billion in goods from

Table 3.2
Japan's trade with Southeast Asia, 1986–90
(In US$ millions)

	Exports					Imports				
	1986	*1987*	*1988*	*1989*	*1990*	*1986*	*1987*	*1988*	*1989*	*1990*
ASEAN										
Brunei	58	40	67	83	86	1,285	1,184	1,117	1,086	1,262
Indonesia	2,662	2,990	3,054	3,301	5,040	7,310	8,427	9,497	11,021	12,721
Malaysia	1,780	2,168	3,060	4,124	5,511	3,846	4,772	4,710	5,107	5,402
Philippines	1,088	1,415	1,740	2,381	2,504	1,221	1,353	2,044	2,059	2,157
Singapore	4,576	6,008	8,311	9,239	10,708	1,463	2,047	2,339	2,952	3,571
Thailand	2,030	2,953	5,162	6,838	9,126	1,391	1,796	2,751	3,583	4,147
Subtotal	12,194	15,574	21,394	25,966	32,975	16,516	19,579	22,458	25,808	29,260
Others										
Myanmar	212	175	184	107	101	49	34	32	34	41
Cambodia	1	1	5	4	5	*	1	1	2	3
Laos	13	15	20	25	20	1	2	7	8	5
Vietnam	191	181	194	167	214	84	145	195	347	595
Total	12,611	15,946	21,797	26,269	33,315	16,650	19,761	22,693	26,199	29,904

* Less than US$1 million.

SOURCE: Japan Tariff Association, *The Summary Report on Trade of Japan* (published monthly).

China in 1990, against exports of US$6.1 billion. However, China's trade with Japan is a surprisingly small part of its overall trade, with two-way trade (including re-exports through Hong Kong) amounting to only 15.1 per cent of China's total trade in 1990, compared to about 30 per cent in 1984.[41]

China's decision to privatize agriculture and focus industrial development on light industry and consumer goods production was highly compatible with Japan's own economic restructuring. Beginning in 1975, Japanese exports increased rapidly under China's liberalized import regime. During the next ten years, the character of Japanese exports shifted from textiles and other light manufactures as China itself began to produce these goods in volume, towards capital goods such as machinery and transport equipment. Meanwhile, Japanese imports of petroleum products dropped in dollar value as oil prices fell, and imports of intermediate goods such as industrial chemicals, steel, and nonferrous metals, textiles and light manufactures rose.[42] Notwithstanding these shifts, value-added remains substantially with Japan.

Due to investor caution, Japan's capital flows to China are dominated by government lending, not private direct investment. As of 31 March 1991 (end of FY 1990), cumulative Japanese investment approvals and notifications totalled US$2.8 billion, second only to Hong Kong and ahead of the United States.[43] Actual investment is probably considerably less due to uncertainties arising out of China's recent political turmoil.

Beginning in the late 1970s, Japan extended large soft loans to China in support of Deng Xiaoping's "Four Modernizations". Japanese aid grew to about US$500 million annually by the mid-1980s, more than four-fifths of it in yen loans. In July 1990, after having suspended aid following the Tiananmen Square massacre, Japan announced its intention at the G-7 meeting to go ahead with the first instalment of a previously committed six-year, US$6 billion (810 billion yen) package of low interest infrastructure development credits from the Overseas Economic Cooperation Fund (OECF).[44] During his August 1991 visit to Beijing, Prime Minister Kaifu said that Japan would release US$940 million (129 billion yen) in soft loans during the current year for infrastructure development projects.[45]

Japan remains highly sensitive to China's importance as a regional power. Considerations concerning China's role in the Northeast Asian balance have, if anything, increased as a result of the decline in U.S.-Soviet tensions and rivalry and Sino-Soviet rapprochement. Tokyo seeks to keep open lines of communication as a way of encouraging Chinese economic modernization and promoting co-operation on key foreign policy issues such as maintaining peace on the Korean peninsula and ending the Cambodian conflict. As discussed in more detail below, Japan has assumed the role of Beijing's principal patron in the face of sanctions imposed by the United States and other Western countries. Notwithstanding Tokyo's sympathetic official policy, Japanese businessmen appear to remain more wary than in the past about their involvement in China.[46]

South Asia

Japan's current role in South Asia is predominantly as an aid donor, not an investor. Despite some breakthroughs, such as Suzuki's joint venture with India's Maruti automobile company, South Asia still accounts for less than one per cent of total Japanese overseas direct investment. Japanese aid to seven South Asian countries totalled US$1.1 billion in 1989, about the same as the United States. Due to the fact that more than half of U.S. aid went to Pakistan alone, Japan was the top donor to all the other countries. Since the United States suspended new economic aid and all military aid to Pakistan in October 1989 because of President Bush's inability to make a congressionally mandated certification that Islamabad does not possess nuclear weapons, Japan has become far and away the dominant donor to the region. Four South Asian nations — India, Pakistan, Bangladesh and Sri Lanka — are in the top ten list of Tokyo's aid recipients.

Prime Minister Kaifu appeared to signal a broadening of Japan's interest in South Asia with his swing through the region in April 1990. Kaifu stressed the role of free markets and democracy in bringing about "a new international order", and emphasized the need for a settlement of the Kashmir issue between India and Pakistan, and for the adoption of domestic economic liberalization measures to attract foreign investment and promote dynamic growth. To hard currency-short India, Kaifu pledged a new concessional loan of 100 billion yen (about US$650 million) for the coming year.[47] In mid-1991, Japan took the lead in arranging financing to cover India's severe balance of payments problems.

While many in the region see Tokyo's aid as a stalking horse for Japanese business interests,[48] Japanese businessmen appear to see the region's low labour costs as overshadowed by poor infrastructure, an unresponsive bureaucracy, and nationalistic policies that discourage foreign investment. For a variety of reasons related to dire economic and financial situations and changing international politics, India, Pakistan and other regional states have made significant moves to attract foreign investment and open up their internal markets to foreign participation, but investment will likely be deterred by political instability and infrastructure overload. Despite these problems, analysts in India and other South Asian countries remain convinced that Tokyo is beginning to focus on South Asia as an area of future investment opportunity if for no other reason than the large size of the potential market.[49] The most recent economic liberalization measures announced by India and Pakistan during 1991 appeared clearly aimed at courting Japanese investors.

Pacific Island states

Both commercial and strategic interests have also prompted a strong surge in Japanese involvement in the newly independent Pacific Island states. Japan's rapidly growing aid to the South Pacific is seen by many as a response both to U.S. calls for greater burden sharing and international ratification of the 1982 Law of the Sea Treaty, which gave states legal control over fishery resources within their 200-mile economic zones. Japan is second after Australia as an aid donor to the region. The US$100 million it disbursed in FY 1989 was more than twice the U.S. economic aid level of US$41.6 million during its partially overlapping FY 1990.[50] Save for substantial loan aid to Papua New Guinea (PNG) and the Solomon Islands, nearly three-fourths of Japan's aid to the South Pacific is in the form of grants, which normally require the procurement of Japanese services and equipment.[51] Japanese companies are also investing heavily in the tourism industry in the island nations. The tourist industry of a number of the islands has been developed almost exclusively by Japanese interests, primarily for use by honeymooners and other Japanese tourists.

Australia and New Zealand

Japan's relationship with Australia focuses primarily on investments in the financial sector, real estate and facilities for Japanese tourists, mining, and local manufacturing for the Australian market. New Zealand, likewise, has emerged as a major focus of tourism development. Strong import-substitution policies in both Australia and New Zealand tend to mandate investment in local manufacturing operations as a requirement for domestic market participation. As the only other developed countries in the region, Australia and New Zealand possess some ability to offer a direct challenge to Japan's aspirations for regional leadership, albeit a limited one.

Japanese investment in Australia, which is heavily concentrated in mining, transportation and tourism-related real estate, totalled about US$16.1 billion as of March 1991, compared to US$14.5 billion for the United States for year end 1990.[52] Cumulative investment in New Zealand is just a fraction of this, at US$925 million. Investment growth in Australasia has been strong in recent years, with three-quarters of total Japanese investment in Australia and more than half of Japan's investment in New Zealand being added since 1985, in nominal dollar terms (Table 2.1). As of 1990, Australia was the largest source of Japanese regional imports (US$12.3 billion), narrowly edging out China, Indonesia, and South Korea, but it was a considerably smaller export market (US$6.9 billion) than Thailand and each of the NIEs. Japan's trade with New Zealand is only a small fraction of its trade with Australia.

Politically, Japan's relations with Australia and New Zealand have elements of tension as well as acknowledged mutuality of interest. Memories of World War II linger amongst the older public, contributing to a contemporary fear of Japanese economic domination. At the same time, government and business leaders in both countries see Japan as a vital export market and as an essential element in their future growth and prosperity.

Partially out of concern about the implications of the U.S.-Canada Free Trade Agreement, agricultural trade friction, and other signs of U.S. tendencies towards "bilateralism", the Hawke government launched a number of initiatives to promote a more activist Australian role in the Asia-Pacific region. These included Prime Minister Hawke's proposal for an Asia-Pacific Economic Cooperation (APEC) entity and efforts in 1990 and 1991 to advance a settlement of the Cambodian conflict.

In its relations with Japan, and its broader economic role in the Asia-Pacific region, Australia will be influenced by its efficient agricultural and resources export sectors, on the one hand, and its relatively inefficient, low-growth, manufacturing sector and comparatively small population base, on the other. The success or failure of current efforts to address macroeconomic problems and other root causes of economic inefficiency are likely to have an important bearing on Australia's ability to play a more vital role in the Asia-Pacific system.

Role of Japan's aid programmes

At present, Japan's aid programmes play a key role in its plans to promote a greater degree of rationalization and co-ordination of Asia-Pacific economic development, with attendant benefits to the Japanese economy. This is hardly a new phenomenon. Japan's aid programmes traditionally have fulfilled a number of foreign and domestic policy objectives. By one account, each phase in Japan's aid strategy has responded to a perceived "vulnerability", with emphasis moving chronologically from promoting exports, to insuring access to vital raw materials, to deflecting foreign criticism of Japan's enormous trade surpluses.[53]

Currently, Japanese aid programmes in the developing parts of the

Asia-Pacific region support twin goals of promoting economic development and stability, on the one hand, and creating infrastructure for the offshore expansion of Japanese business, on the other. Japanese officials and government agencies have developed a number of concepts for better integrating the region, especially Southeast Asia, into the Japanese economy through the development of infrastructure and the transfer of technical and manufacturing know-how, with the broad objective of promoting economic modernization along lines that complement the Japanese economy. Recently, Japan has cautiously added other goals such as promoting democratization and human rights, but the seriousness of its intent in this regard is still being questioned, and in any event Tokyo's outlook on these issues will remain considerably different from that of the United States and other Western donors.

Southeast Asian focus of Japan's ODA

Japan has continued to be a substantial aid donor to the ASEAN countries even while they move towards middle-income status and their raw materials acquire relatively less significance to the Japanese economy. In fact, three Southeast Asian countries — Indonesia, Thailand and the Philippines — are among the top five recipients of Japanese ODA. The current leading recipient, Indonesia, receives about US$2 billion in Japanese ODA and Export-Import Bank credits each year, a critical factor in servicing its US$41 billion foreign debt — more than a third of which is owed to Japanese lenders or the Japanese Government.[54]

Japan's importance to Southeast Asian countries as a multilateral aid donor also has been growing strongly. Japan is the dominant force in the Asian Development Bank (ADB), whose director customarily is Japanese, and the major resort of Southeast Asian countries with critical balance of payments problems. For instance, Tokyo committed US$1.6 billion out of a total of US$3.7 billion in commitments for 1989 under the framework of the nineteen-nation Philippine Assistance Program (PAP), also known as the Multilateral Aid Initiative (MAI) for the Philippines, and US$1.3 billion for 1990. Both years' pledges amount to 40 per cent or more of the total and are ten times as large as the U.S. share for this period.[55]

Minkatsu and the New Aid Plan

The *minkatsu* concept, loosely translated as "utilization of private vitality", involves the recycling of both surplus Japanese capital and high labour content manufacturing capacity to low wage developing countries. The so-called New Asian Industries Development Plan, otherwise known as the New Aid Plan, sponsored by the export-oriented Ministry of International Trade and Industry epitomizes the *minkatsu* concept. The plan involves a complex blend of private and official capital flows to help countries develop an industrialization strategy, build infrastructure such as ports, roads and power plants, and enhance local technical and management standards. It has been portrayed as "at the cutting edge of Japan's initiative to organize the industrial integration of East and South-East Asia", and a key tool "to keep Japan's flock [of geese] in formation".[56]

The large number of Japanese agencies and institutions involved in the New Aid Plan gives every appearance of a highly co-ordinated effort. Contributing organizations include the Overseas Economic Co-operation Foundation, which provides yen loans for infrastructure projects, the Export-Import (Ex-Im) Bank, which gives loans to private Japanese firms as well as foreign firms and enterprises, the Japan International Cooperation Agency (JICA), which provides technical assistance, and the Japan External Trade Organization (JETRO), which promotes trade and investment. Other involved bureaucratic organizations include the Association for Overseas Technological Scholarships (AOTS) and Japan-ASEAN centres which send trainees to Japan.[57]

ASEAN-Japan Development Fund

The ASEAN-Japan Development Fund (AJDF), announced by former Prime Minister Takeshita at the Manila ASEAN summit in 1987, has been the main manifestation thus far of the New Aid Plan. Significantly, and in keeping with an established tradition, Takeshita announced the plan on his first official overseas trip as Prime Minister. Under the AJDF, the Japanese Government has set aside US$2 billion to promote the establishment of joint business ventures in the ASEAN countries. Lending practices by the AJDF in Malaysia, its main focus to date, have generated severe criticism from Japan's partners in the G-7 group of industrialized countries and from the World Bank and the IMF, which have claimed that in the name of assuming a greater aid "burden" Japan is providing subsidized loans to facilitate Japanese industrial expansion into Southeast Asia.[58]

Whether this picture of a strategic plan for integrating Southeast Asia into the Japanese economy is alarmist or realistic is difficult to answer with any certainty. There can be no doubt that Japanese investment is burgeoning in countries such as Thailand and Malaysia that have worked most closely with Japanese officials to carry out pro-industrialization policy changes. At the same time, Japanese interest in any country appears to be highly dependent on factor costs and the availability of necessary infrastructure such as roads, ports and electric power. Japanese multinationals and their bureaucratic allies are primarily interested in expanding or maintaining their world-wide market shares, not the creation of a new "co-prosperity sphere". At present, Southeast Asian countries themselves appear to be more anxious about losing out in the competition to attract new investment, whether from Japan or elsewhere, than about economic domination.[59]

The aid-trade nexus

Commercial orientation of Japan's aid programmes

Although Japan has reduced the formally "tied" element of its aid programmes to the lowest level among the OECD donors, its aid programmes still play a significant role in promoting its exports. According to one source, for a five year period during the early and mid-1980s some 60 per cent of Japan's "untied" loans overall resulted in procurement of Japanese goods and services, while 85 per cent of "untied" loans to the Less Developed Countries (LDCs) resulted in procurement in Japan.[60]

Much like American aid programmes in the 1950s and 1960s, Japanese aid tends to support capital intensive projects such as building ports, power plants and telecommunication facilities that characteristically have high import content. In addition, the "recipient-initiated request" basis of Japan's aid programmes gives strong advantages to its engineering and construction firms in the field, who are able to develop project proposals and suggest them to the host government. The fact that grant aid that often constitutes the seed money for such engineering studies is almost always tied, the sometime use of "LDC untied" loans in which only developing countries' firms can compete with Japanese companies, and the cosy relationship between Japanese engineering consulting firms and the powerful international trade and industry (MITI), construction and transport ministries, further tip the scales towards Japanese businesses.[61]

For better or worse, government-provided or guaranteed concessional loans remain the coinage of competition for large, developing country infrastructure projects — a fact that the United States is beginning to come to terms with.[62] Examples abound, such as Mitsui trading company's contract for constructing a 1,000 watt thermal power plant in northern India financed by a US$600 million OECF loan. In general, such projects are closed to U.S. and European bids. Reportedly, virtually all of Japan's US$2 billion in OECF soft loans to South Asia ("Southwest Asia" in Japanese parlance) involved infrastructure projects closed to companies from other developed countries.[63]

The longer-term market penetration aspects of Japan's infrastructure lending programmes may be even more significant than the immediate export potential of Japanese aid projects. The participation of Japanese companies in infrastructure projects also establishes their technology as the standard and facilitates the development of follow-on business.[64] All other things being equal, the less developed the region, the more the potential return on getting in on the "ground floor". In fact, the European countries are even more aggressive purveyors of commercially oriented aid, but their relatively weak market position in Asia means that the overall impact of such lending by France, Britain or Italy pales into insignificance compared to that of Japan.

Efforts at aid reform

Largely as a result of outside pressure, Japan is moving slowly to reduce the commercial bias of its aid programme. In response to criticisms from the United States, the OECD and recipient countries, Japanese aid officials have countered with a strong defence of their approach and a denial of undue commercial motivations, even while acknowledging some of the (non-commercialist) criticisms as valid.[65] An English language summary of the overview to the annual White Paper, *Japan's ODA, 1991*, acknowledges, for instance, that Japan's ODA "is still low, when measured according to recognized international criteria, such as the ratio of aid to GNP (0.31 per cent), grant share and grant element".[66] On the other hand, Japan strongly rejects commercialization criticisms. Official documents cite a drop in ODA loans resulting in contracts for Japanese firms from 75 per cent in FY 1984 to 38 per cent in 1989, while shares of business going to LDC contractors have risen to 41 per cent.[67]

To date, these rebuttals remain less than persuasive. First, while the growth in contracts for European and U.S. firms represents a clear opening up of the system, the growth of LDC contractor shares remains suspect. It is not yet clear that the rising share of business acquired by LDC contractors represents a genuine growth in local procurement or just increased participation by Japanese offshore subsidiaries or Japanese-controlled joint ventures. Second, the blending of ODA with other export credits still provides great advantages to Japanese contractors and exporters, since Export-Import Bank type credits normally require procurement from Japanese vendors.

The obstacles to reform are formidable. Policymaking responsibility remains divided among four agencies and ministries whose institutional aims differ considerably and who jealously guard their "turf". Achieving a consensus in favour of a more open aid process involves the subordination of vested interests to broader policy goals, never an easy task in any country, least of all Japan. In addition, the main political constituency for expanding aid budgets lies in the business community itself, whose interests would be harmed by more altruistic aid policies. As a consequence, critics remain convinced that politically powerful business interests will continue to seek ways to maintain a significant commercial focus in Japan's ODA.

ASEAN focus of new Japanese investment in Asia

Although the NIEs, especially South Korea and Taiwan, were the first targets of Japanese offshore manufacturing investment in Asia, rising costs of labour and other inputs in the NIEs have caused a relative shift of investment into the developing countries of Southeast Asia. Since FY 1988, investment in the ASEAN countries — including Singapore — has consistently exceeded investment in the three East Asian NIEs and by substantially increasing margins.

A variety of factors have come together to create this surge of Japanese offshore investment into Southeast Asia. Various "pull" factors include favourable local policies relating to economic liberalization and rising regional incomes and growing consumer markets. Equally important have been the "push" effects of *endaka*, the growing labour shortage in Japan, and a similar change in comparative advantage in previous areas of Japanese investment such as South Korea and Taiwan.

Due to their particular roles and geographic locations, Hong Kong and Singapore have shared in the exponential rise in Southeast Asian investment rather than the relative decline in Japanese investment experienced by their fellow NIEs, South Korea and Taiwan, since about 1987. Hong Kong has attracted portfolio and real estate investment, as well as serving as an entry point for investment in Guandong and other Chinese coastal provinces. Singapore has similarly benefited from its favourable geographic location in the fast-growing Southeast Asian market and its aggressive economic restructuring policies. The significance of the sharp decline in new investment in Singapore in FY 1990 compared with the previous year remains to be seen. (Ironically, U.S.

investment in Singapore *rose* by US$1.65 billion during calendar 1990, the steepest rise in many years.[68])

Although the impetus for the post-*endaka* surge of Japanese manufacturing investment in Southeast Asia may have been to maintain a competitive edge in the global markets in the face of the sharply higher yen, analysts increasingly regard Japanese investment interest in the ASEAN countries as targeted on the growing regional market. As one analyst has noted, "Japan's direct investment in Southeast Asia is increasingly driven by the objective of establishing strategic control of the megamarkets of the next decade".[69] Partly as a consequence, a general decline in overseas investment arising out of the post-1990 financial crisis has not been as marked in Southeast Asia as in other areas. This continued relative strength of investment in ASEAN underscores Japanese confidence in the growth prospects of the region and the key role that manufacturing investment in Southeast Asia plays in Japan's global competitiveness.

Thailand has been the most favoured Japanese investment target in the past few years, followed by Malaysia. According to the Thai Board of Investment, Japan accounted for 53 per cent of all foreign investment in Thailand as of early 1990.[70] Thailand's duty-free access to the U.S. market under the Generalized System of Preferences (GSP), its relatively large domestic market, favourable economic policies, and comparatively low wage rates initially attracted Japanese investors. Recently, growing problems of power shortages, transportation bottlenecks and other indicators of insufficient infrastructure have prompted a shift of focus towards Malaysia and Indonesia. From a much lower base, Japanese investment has been growing rapidly even in the politically troubled Philippines.

Japanese investment has played a key role in sustaining Malaysia's rapid GNP growth, which averaged 9.2 per cent during 1988–90. Significantly, for a country that used to be a primary-resources exporter, manufactured goods largely originating in Japanese and other multinational plants constituted 60.4 per cent of total exports in 1990.[71] Japanese investment in Malaysia, often in joint ventures with companies controlled by Prime Minister Mahathir's United Malays National Organization (UMNO) party, totalled US$3.2 billion as of March 1991

Table 3.3

Japan's direct investment in ASEAN, FY 1985–91

(In US$ millions)

	FY 1985	FY 1986	FY 1987	FY 1988	FY 1989	FY 1990	Total 31 March 1991
ASEAN	936	856	1,524	2,713	4,684	4,082	27,437
Brunei	1	1	—	—	—	—	109
Indonesia	408	250	545	586	631	1,105	11,540
Malaysia	79	158	163	387	673	725	3,231
Philippines	61	21	72	134	202	258	1,580
Singapore	339	302	494	747	1,902	840	6,555
Thailand	48	124	250	859	1,276	1,154	4,422
Reference comparison							
China	100	226	1,226	296	438	349	2,823
Hong Kong	131	502	1,072	1,662	1,898	1,785	9,850
South Korea	134	436	647	483	606	284	4,138
Taiwan	114	291	367	372	494	446	2,731

SOURCE: Ministry of Finance, "Monthly Statistics of Governmental Finance and Money", No. 452, 19 December 1989.

(Table 3.3). Until recently, the greater part of Japanese investment was in the electronics industry.[72] Since the Gulf war, Japan has begun to increase its role in developing Malaysia's oil and gas industry.

Japan's interest in Indonesia, with its nearly 200 million people, is both strategic and economic. According to one source, Indonesia supplies Japan with 96 per cent of its plywood, 53 per cent of its natural gas, 44 per cent of its sawn timber and 13 per cent of its crude oil.[73] Based on past investments in Indonesia's petroleum and other natural-resources based industries and fast increasing investment in the manufacturing sector, cumulative investment now totals US$11.5 billion, or about 42 per cent of Japan's total investment in the six ASEAN countries.

As a sign of Japanese confidence in Indonesia, investment in FY 1990 was nearly twice that of FY 1989 in the face of a levelling off elsewhere, and the largest in any ASEAN country (Table 3.3). Japanese companies have found investment in Indonesia increasingly attractive as a result of favourable wage levels and policy decisions liberalizing the terms for foreign participation in the economy including, most recently, banking. Due to continuing limits on foreign equity, Japanese investment in Indonesia tends to take the form of loans to joint-venture partners of Japanese companies.

The investment-trade nexus

Even more than Japanese aid programmes, the surge of direct investment has fuelled Japanese exports and promoted a significant restructuring of intra-Asian trade relationships. Thus far, Japanese investment has tended to promote a kind of triangular trade pattern rather than a proportional enhancement of Japan's bilateral trade with host countries. In effect, as a result of offshore investment, Japan has shifted a part of its trade surplus with the United States into other countries' accounts. As of 1987, nearly 85 per cent of the manufacturing output of Japanese affiliates in Asia were still destined for the local market or third countries, notably the United States, and only 15.8 per cent were destined for Japan (Table 3.4).

Emerging trade patterns show both growing vertical linkages between

Table 3.4
Input-output analysis of Japanese offshore production
in the Asia-Pacific region
(Percentages)

Region	1981 Mfg.	1981 Non-Mfg.	1984 Mfg.	1984 Non-Mfg	1987 Mfg.	1987 Non-Mfg.
Inputs: Source of						
Japanese companies' parts and components						
Asia						
Local	42.2	30.2	44.7	40.3	42.9	54.7
Japan	41.5	45.1	38.4	26.5	45.3	28.2
3rd country	16.3	47.5	16.9	33.1	12.6	53.5
Oceania*						
Local	19.5	58.3	33.0	29.4	31.4	26.1
Japan	60.9	33.5	65.3	58.1	65.5	65.4
3rd country	19.6	8.2	1.7	12.5	3.1	8.5
Outputs: Destination of						
Japanese companies' offshore production						
Asia						
Local	63.9	31.6	66.9	43.3	54.7	33.8
Japan	9.8	45.1	10.8	34.0	15.8	24.7
3rd country	26.4	23.3	22.3	22.8	29.9	41.5
Oceania*						
Local	80.6	34.6	81.6	52.3	83.5	60.5
Japan	80.6	34.6	81.6	52.3	83.5	60.5
3rd country	5.6	13.4	2.2	8.9	1.8	13.7

* Australasia and the Pacific Islands.

SOURCE: Compiled from Japan Development Bank, *Deepened Inter-national Linkages Among Pan-Pacific Countries: Trades Foreign Direct Investment and Technology Transfer.* No. 138, February 1990 (in Japanese). Tables III-22 and III-24, pp. 108 and 110.

Japanese parent companies and their offshoot subsidiaries or joint partners, and horizontal linkages among Japanese-controlled offshore manufacturing facilities. The vertical linkages reflect the tight relationships of Japanese multinationals and their offshore subsidiaries, including the extensive use of critical components made in Japan. The linkages at present are dominated by Japanese exports of capital goods and components which, in most countries, dwarf any return flow of manufactured goods or sub-assemblies.

The functioning of the unique Japanese *keiretsu* system, which is characterized by families of companies — including banks, trading companies, multinational manufacturing companies and their parts suppliers — holding each other's stock, tends to enhance the integrative effect of Japanese business operations in the region. Automobile assembly plants bring in their wake component suppliers such as Asahi Glass and Bridgestone Tires, which have subsidiaries in Southeast Asian countries, leading to what some call a "complementation" scheme with benefits for both the ASEAN countries and Japan.[74] More or less the same pattern holds true to the operations of Japanese electronics companies, which carry out production and assembly operations on a multi-country, regional basis.

Despite policies of recipient countries aimed at raising the local content of foreign-owned production, the increasing use of Southeast Asia as an assembly base appears actually to be causing the proportion of parts and components in local manufacturing operations that come from Japan to increase. The share of Japanese components utilized in Japanese-owned plants in Asia rose from 38.4 per cent in 1984 to 45.3 per cent in 1987, after an earlier decline.

Balance sheet on Japan's economic role

Stimulus to regional economic integration

The tendency of Japanese companies to produce components in various sites around the region according to each country's comparative advantages has also been a powerful force for regional economic integration.

Table 3.5
Japan's imports of manufactured goods by
region and country
(In US$ millions and percentages)

Region/Country	1985	1986	1987	1988	1989	1990
World						
Amount	40,157	52,781	65,961	91,838	106,140	118,028
Growth rate	−1.1	31.4	25.0	39.2	15.6	11.2
E. Asian NIEs (3)						
Amount	5,234	7,200	11,596	17,047	18,844	17,242
Growth	−1.0	37.6	61.1	47.0	9.5	−8.5
ASEAN						
Growth	1,853	2,086	3,083	4,592	6,650	7,648
Growth rate	0.3	12.6	47.8	48.9	44.8	15.0
China						
Growth	1,751	1,969	2,941	4,641	5,634	6,119
Growth rate	22.1	12.5	49.3	57.8	21.4	8.6

SOURCE: Ministry of Finance data made available by the Japan External
Trade Organization.

It has been argued that the growth of horizontal trade among Japanese offshore subsidiaries may be doing more to promote intra-regional trade than any steps taken by ASEAN during the whole of its existence. The regionalization of production in Southeast Asia has greatly boosted intra-ASEAN trade, which reached US$50 billion in 1990. This phenomenon has been most evident in the automotive and electronics sectors. Similar patterns have developed as the result of growing NIEs investment as well. In the words of one Southeast Asian economist, "willing or not, the ASEAN economies definitely have become an integral part of a production structure that is emerging in the Pacific region, with Japan as its core".[75]

Increasing imports of Asian manufactured goods

Although Japanese FDI tends to promote exports from Japan — especially in the early phases of an investment project — it also contributes to rising imports of manufactured goods from Asian countries. The *value* of imports of manufactured goods from the Asian NIEs, the ASEAN countries and China grew from US$8.8 billion in 1985 to US$31 billion in 1990 (Table 3.5). The share of manufactured goods in the total import mix has also risen rapidly. Some 77.1 per cent of Japan's imports from the NIEs were manufactured goods as of 1990. From a much lower base, the proportion of manufactured goods in Japan's imports from the ASEAN countries more than quadrupled during the period 1980–90, from 6.1 per cent in the beginning of the decade to 27.3 per cent at the end (Table 3.6).

Continuing inequality in trade ties with Japan

It is less encouraging, however, that trade ties between Japan and most Asia-Pacific countries remain unequal. Not only does Japan maintain large and growing surpluses with most Asia-Pacific trade partners, but Japanese companies tend to dominate both sides of the trade equation. According to one account, most of the growth of manufactured exports to Japan, especially consumer electronics goods from the NIEs, "have mainly consisted of goods made by, or produced under contract for, big Japanese companies".[76] Local producers still find it very hard to crack the Japanese market. Most of the trade of Southeast Asian countries with Japan is carried on between local Japanese affiliates and their parents, or by Japanese trading companies. Access to the Japanese market by indigenously controlled Southeast Asian manufacturing companies appears negligible.

Competitive pressures on the East Asian NIEs

The growing competitiveness problems of the East Asian NIEs that have emerged in the past two years underscore the unevenly divided

Table 3.6
Proportion of manufactured goods in Japan's imports
(Percentge share)

	World	East Asian NIEs (3)	ASEAN (5)
1980	22.8	50.8	6.1
1981	24.8	56.8	6.3
1982	24.9	56.5	6.1
1983	27.2	55.5	7.5
1984	29.8	57.1	8.4
1985	31.0	57.8	9.2
1986	41.8	62.3	12.6
1987	44.1	66.2	15.8
1988	48.9	72.9	20.1
1989	50.3	77.9	26.9
1990	50.2	77.1	27.3

SOURCE: Government of Japan, Ministry of Finance
Customs statistics. Supplemented by other
MOF data for 1989–90.

benefits of the "flying geese" model. Based partly on earlier Japanese investment and technology transfers and the rapid rise of the yen after 1985, imports from the East Asian NIEs started to rise rapidly. Japanese consumers began to show more sensitivity to price differentials. Japanese imports of manufactured goods from Hong Kong, South Korea and Taiwan grew by 37.6 per cent in 1986 and an astounding 61.1 per cent in 1987 (Table 3.5). Subsequently, the upward revaluation of the South Korean and Taiwanese currencies, rising costs and resurgent Japanese competitiveness led to a reversal of these trends. The annual rate of growth of manufactures exported to Japan from the three East Asian NIEs fell to 9.5 per cent in 1989 and registered negative growth of −8.5 per cent in 1990. These trends are shown graphically in Figures 3.1 and 3.2.

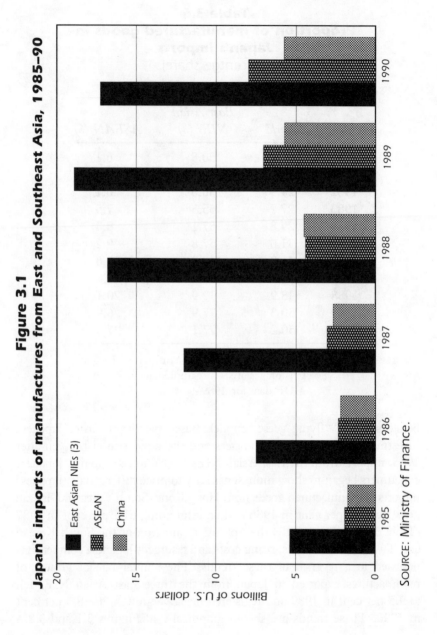

Figure 3.1

Japan's imports of manufactures from East and Southeast Asia, 1985–90

SOURCE: Ministry of Finance.

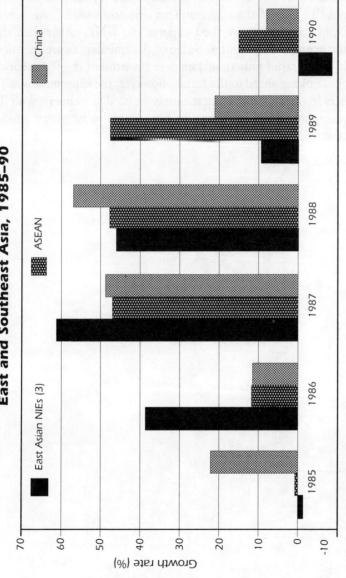

Figure 3.2
Growth of Japan's imports of manufactures from East and Southeast Asia, 1985–90

SOURCE: Ministry of Finance.

For the time being, most countries in the region tend to emphasize the positive side of their economic relationship with Japan, including the rapid absolute rise in their exports and GNP, rather than the continuing economic inequities. Some of the imbalances are the inevitable result of the rapid growth of Japanese investment in offshore manufacturing. Looking ahead to the future, however, the expectations of Japan's partners in the region may increasingly be hard to reconcile with Tokyo's own economic goals, and may, in time, come to be major obstacles to Japanese aspirations of regional leadership.

4
Japan's growing political and diplomatic role

Cautious but steady growth of Japanese activism

After years of avoiding the political limelight, Japan is moving cautiously but steadily to play a political and diplomatic role more commensurate with its economic strength. In the words of former Prime Minister Toshiki Kaifu during his April–May 1991 trip to Southeast Asia, Japan "now hopes to play an appropriate role in the political sphere as a nation of peace".[77] The government of Prime Minister Kiichi Miyazawa has shown an even more ambitious attitude towards projecting Japan into the Asian and global political arena. Evidence of Japan's growing activism can be found in numerous diplomatic and regional leadership initiatives over the past several years. Less clear are the goals of Japanese activism, the ability of the Japanese political system to support a larger role, and the extent to which Japan's leadership will be accepted by other Asia-Pacific countries.

To date, Japan has pursued its expanded role within the framework of global partnership with the United States. Beneath the reality of close co-ordination and substantial policy agreement between Tokyo and Washington, however, lies another reality of a steady shift of power and influence in Japan's direction and increasing Japanese policy divergence. At almost every point in time, Japan has preferred that the United States take the lead on issues relating to the stability of the region, but it has indicated a willingness to take the initiative when necessary to protect its interests and further its own agenda. This process is most apparent in Southeast Asia, and is increasingly evident in policies towards China and the Korean peninsula.

In one sense, Japan's current diplomatic activism, and the balance between its economic and political roles in the region follow a long established pattern. Japanese Prime Ministers have been conducting personal diplomacy in the region for decades, normally, as now, amidst scepticism and with doubtful effect.[78] In another sense, as in the case of Japan's economic role, Tokyo's impact is now in a different class. Japan has moved from being a supporting player in a U.S. dominated Asia-Pacific system to an acknowledged regional leader with the ability and — increasingly — the will to act independently.

Evolution of
Japan's post-war political-diplomatic role

Early reliance on the United States

Precisely because of the consequences of Japan's earlier adventurism and World War II defeat, Tokyo long subordinated its regional policy to the needs of the U.S.-Japan relationship. However painful the process may have been psychologically, dependence on the United States worked to the advantage of Japan's post-war economic revival and international rehabilitation. The United States deliberately promoted Japan's re-entry into the Asian economic and political system through aid to its industrial recovery, support for its participation in the 1954 Colombo Plan, and backing for the establishment of the Asian Development Bank (ADB), in which Japan has exercised a predominant influence from its founding in 1966.[79] These initiatives were part of an overall U.S. strategy to undercut leftist radicalism in Japan and otherwise promote regional economic growth as a barrier to the spread of Communism.

During the 1950s and 1960s, Japan played a largely economic role in Asia, despite some ventures in personal diplomacy by Japanese leaders. Export credits provided to the resource-rich countries of Southeast Asia under the rubric of war "reparations" helped to restore ties with former victims of Japanese aggression and helped to rebuild Japan's own manufacturing industries. Politically, Japan operated distinctly under the shadow of U.S. influence.

The so-called Nixon "shocks" of the early 1970s started a gradual process of rethinking Japan's expectations of the United States. The *shoku*, as the Japanese called them, which included ending the convertibility of gold, embargoing soybean exports and initiating a secret opening to China, directly threatened major Japanese economic and political interests. They had the effect of putting Japanese leaders on notice that Washington's unchallenged economic freedom of action had come to an end, and that Japan's own interests were likely to suffer as U.S. leaders gave primacy to their own domestic political interests and the needs of maintaining an acceptable geostrategic balance with the former Soviet Union.

The Fukuda Doctrine and other responses to the American withdrawal from Indochina

The fall of Saigon in 1975 even more profoundly disturbed Japanese leaders and prompted a series of cautious efforts to fill the vacuum left by the U.S. withdrawal from Indochina. Both the Japan-ASEAN forum, launched in March 1977, and the August 1977 proclamation of the Fukuda Doctrine were aimed at helping to stabilize Southeast Asia and to reassure Vietnam's non-Communist neighbours. The Fukuda Doctrine embodied three principles: rejection of a Japanese military role; "heart-to-heart" understanding with Southeast Asian countries; and equal partnership with the ASEAN countries in their efforts to contain Vietnam.[80] Tokyo first tried to attract Hanoi from its expansionist policy by offers of economic aid, but following the Vietnamese invasion of Cambodia, Japan aligned itself with ASEAN's strong condemnation of Vietnamese aggression.[81]

In the late 1970s, Japan's emergence as an economic superpower and evidence that the United States was losing the ability to sustain its role as the dominant military and economic power in the region caused Japanese leaders to adopt more ambitious foreign and defence policy goals. Many of Japan's moves, such as the defence buildup that began with the 1976 National Defense Program Outline (NDPO), stemmed both from American prodding and Japanese anxiety about U.S. staying power. Japanese leaders were especially troubled by the 1977 plan of the Carter Administration to withdraw American ground forces from South Korea by 1982, a step that was never fully implemented due to Asian and domestic U.S. opposition and changing international conditions.

Search for Comprehensive National Security

Japan shared the surprise and alarm of the United States at the Soviet invasion of Afghanistan in December 1979, and a general sense of heightened threats to stability from the Soviet Union and its allies in Asia — Vietnam and North Korea. The indications of reawakened Soviet expansionism proved especially troubling due to the corresponding perception that the United States was steadily losing the economic wherewithal and political will to carry out its traditional post-war role of shoring up non-Communist Asian governments and providing a security shield for Japan. A blue ribbon Comprehensive National Security Study Group framed the issue in explicit terms in its July 1980 report to Acting Prime Minister Masayoshi Ito (following the death of Prime Minister Ohira). The document, still cited as a fundamental policy blueprint by the Defense Agency, called attention to the "termination of clear American supremacy in both military and economic spheres" and sketched out a series of steps both to strengthen self-reliance and reinforce the credibility of the U.S. nuclear umbrella through increased co-operation.[82]

In keeping with its emphasis on "comprehensive security", the report outlined various ways that Japan could promote its military, security, and economic well-being, including playing "a major role" in promoting economic development and "the formation of orderly North-South relations" and contributing to the maintenance and management of the international system". At the political and military level, these goals were to be pursued through greater military self-reliance, and a political strategy of seeking relations with the Soviet Union and China that would, on the one hand, promote U.S.-Japan solidarity against aggressive actions while, on the other, not unnecessarily provoke hostility against Japan. At the economic level, Japan would promote energy and food security, in part through closer relations with producer nations, and support agricultural development and the adoption of free market policies in developing countries.

The document pointedly took issue with the conventional wisdom that confrontation could be defused by "peace and diplomacy" alone, or that the causes of conflict could be removed by economic co-operation. Rather, it stressed that in a continuum of means to promote security, "every country, as a matter of course, gives weight to military means in coping with the question of military security". Even more boldly, the document advanced the idea that even in matters of non-military security — such as energy dependence — resort to military means could not be totally discounted.

In line with this approach, the Japanese Government undertook a major buildup of its Self-Defense Forces and accepted responsibility for defending the sea approaches to Japan out to 1,000 nautical miles, in an arc that included the Philippines and adjacent Southeast Asian waters. Japan provided a large amount of credit to South Korea in support of Seoul's FY 1982–86 five-year development plan. In support of Deng Xiaoping's modernization programme, Japan made China, with whom it had normalized relations in 1978, its number one aid recipient, temporarily displacing Indonesia from top ranking. Japan also provided increased aid to Pakistan and Thailand under the rubric of "countries bordering areas of conflict".

The much publicized Ron-Yasu relationship between Prime Minister Yasuhiro Nakasone and President Ronald Reagan underscored the growing sense of partnership in U.S.-Japan relations in the early 1980s. Japan tacitly backed the stiffened U.S. military and diplomatic response to Soviet adventurism and agreed to a limited role in the American Strategic Defense Initiative (SDI), the so-called "Star Wars" space-based anti-missile defence programme. Japan maintained an active interest in the Afghan conflict under Nakasone's successor, Prime

Minister Noboru Takeshita, and later agreed to participate in monitoring the 1988 Soviet troop withdrawal from Afghanistan.

Emerging regional activism

Endaka and rising Japanese foreign policy activism

By the mid and late 1980s, Japan began to flex its economic muscles in pursuit of a U.S-Japan relationship that would provide greater recognition of Tokyo's perspectives. What had been a gradual and tentative rise of Japan as a major actor in Asia-Pacific affairs began to accelerate, largely as a result of Japan's swelling trade surpluses and the mirror-image financial and economic weakness in the United States. Although the departure of Nakasone had removed a source of high-profile international leadership, underlying economic factors and bureaucratic continuity tended to propel Japan forward. Prime Minister Noboru Takeshita, who took office in late 1987, surprised many with his early plunge into international diplomacy. In part, Takeshita's confidence stemmed from strong support from his "handlers" in the Ministry of Foreign Affairs, who had already institutionalized many facets of Nakasone's activism.

Although Japan continues to send somewhat mixed signals and demonstrate characteristic caution, a pattern is starting to emerge of an overall leadership plan. Without abandoning broad shared objectives and without directly undercutting U.S. policy, Japan has partially broken ranks with the United States on a number of Asian policy issues. These include, especially, its aid policies towards China, Myanmar and the Philippines. Moreover, it has at the same time expanded its horizons to include more active diplomacy across a the broad sweep of the Asia rimland including the Indian subcontinent, Indochina, and its immediate neighbours, the two Koreas, China and the former U.S.S.R.

Pursuit of regional stability and economic goals

As it has for most of the post-war period, current Japanese regional policy emphasizes the twin goals of support for a stable regional environment and the promotion of its commercial interests. The range of initiatives has included diplomatic efforts to broker a political settlement of the Cambodian conflict; the use of economic incentives to promote the incorporation of the countries of Indochina and Myanmar into the market-led ASEAN development pattern; support for liberalization in China and Beijing's integration into the global economy; moves to strengthen official ties to South Korea while simultaneously opening up contacts aimed at promoting normalization with North Korea; and hard-nosed negotiations with Moscow to regain the so-called Northern Territories and create favourable conditions for Japanese participation in the development of the former Soviet Far East. In early 1991, in response to criticism from the United States and other Western countries of its reaction to the Persian Gulf crisis, and out of its own concern about the destabilizing spread of nuclear and missile proliferation in the Middle East and Asia, the Kaifu government also announced its intention to take into account levels of arms spending by developing countries when deciding on ODA levels.

Kaifu's articulation of Japan's world view

Former Prime Minister Toshiki Kaifu actively promoted Japan's more ambitious world view in a series of trips to other Asian countries, starting with a precedent-setting trip to South Asia in April 1990. In an address to the Indian Parliament that was billed as a major policy speech, and which seemed to signal an expansion of Japan's geopolitical horizon in Asia, Prime Minister Kaifu sketched out a "new international order" which emphasizes free markets and democracy. He asserted that Japan can and must play a positive role by putting to effective use its economic and technological capabilities.[83]

A trip by Kaifu to five ASEAN countries in late April and early May 1991 appeared to be explicitly geared towards offsetting the political damage arising from Japan's timid response to the Persian Gulf crisis and indicating Tokyo's intention to act as an Asian power. In his keynote speech in Singapore (an alternative venue chosen after the Thai coup in Bangkok), Kaifu sketched out a Japanese world view in which the end of the Cold War had unleashed potential new threats to peace and security arising from religious, ethnic, territorial and other causes. He stressed Japan's desire to play a major international role in this "transitional period", not militarily, but through the application of its economic power and influence. In this respect, he sought to defuse any concerns about the transit of four minesweepers through Southeast Asian waters en route to the Gulf, which coincided with his visit.

In his Singapore address, Kaifu also called attention to the growing importance of Japan, the Newly Industrializing Economies and the ASEAN countries in the emerging world order, and asserted the need for Japan and its neighbours to "go beyond the economic realm and work in [the] political, social and foreign policy realms as well to become a major force for stability grounded in freedom and democracy". The experience of the Gulf war notwithstanding, Kaifu asserted that military power was becoming less important than "the sum total of economic strength, scientific and technological prowess, social stability and order, and the whole range of other factors that constitute the influence of a country".

Kaifu unabashedly indicated Japan's intention to focus primarily on its own region, and he positioned Tokyo in qualified support of regional economic co-operation. ASEAN and the rest of Asia, he said, will continue to be the priority focus of Japan's ODA. He acknowledged Singapore Prime Minister Goh Chok Tong's concept of a "Crescent of Prosperity" linking ASEAN, Indochina and Northeast Asia, as well as Malaysian Prime Minister Mahathir's initiative for an East Asian Economic Group (EAEG), but with the important caveat, in regard to the latter, that any such regional grouping should be based on forestalling new moves towards protectionism and promoting co-operation with the rest of the world.

Although he strongly asserted Japan's intention to play a leadership role in efforts to address regional problems, the Prime Minister indirectly underscored Tokyo's continued dependence on its security relationship with the United States to provide cover for Japan's regional role. "The issues of peace and prosperity in the Asia-Pacific region," he said, "cannot be realistically discussed without a U.S. role." As in the Gulf region, he found the U.S. presence "an important stabilizing factor not only in the military sphere but in the political sense as well".

Japan's increasingly independent course on China

Japan's response to the suppression of pro-democracy movements in China typifies the mix of motives activating Japanese policy as well as the range of policy tools available to Tokyo. Apparent goals include a desire to accommodate strong pressures from Japanese business interests, a perceived need for broad solidarity with the United States and other Western countries in promoting economic and political liberalization, and concern about maintaining regional stability and preventing the isolation of beleaguered regimes.

Following the Tiananmen Square massacre, Japan has acted in support of several high priority concerns, apart from its obvious commercial interests. Japan has sought to encourage China to continue its economic modernization and openness to the global economy, notwithstanding its political retrogression. Japan has also acted to protect its broader political stake in good relations with China, and in particular to prevent being whipsawed by abrupt shifts in U.S. policy towards Beijing or being caught off guard by U.S. moves such as the selective resumption of high-technology sales. Finally, Japan has seemed concerned to make sure that actions against China did not rebound against efforts to promote a settlement of the Cambodian conflict.

In its pursuit of these goals, Japan has partially broken ranks with the United States and, in the process, emerged as a more influential force in shaping Southeast Asian reactions as well. Japan initially joined the Western countries in suspending aid credits following Beijing's June 1989 bloody suppression of the pro-democracy movement, but Japanese leaders soon grew alarmed at the consequences of Western sanctions on the outlook of China's leaders. At the July 1990 ASEAN foreign ministers summit in Brunei, and the subsequent Japan-ASEAN dialogue meeting, Japan's then Foreign Minister, Horishi Mitsuzuka, warned that isolating China at the risk of driving it closer to the Soviet

Union "may not be a wise policy". According to some accounts, Japan was instrumental in getting ASEAN to take a moderate stance on the situation, especially since the U.S. Secretary of State, James Baker, did not raise the China issue in his own speech.[84]

Shortly thereafter, at the July 1990 meeting of the G-7 industrialized countries, Japan succeeded in winning agreement on communique language permitting modifications of the aid sanctions in response to changing conditions. This was aimed at opening the way for the resumption of World Bank loans for basic human needs and economic reform, including infrastructure projects, and a partial lifting of Japan's own sanctions. In late 1990, Japan and China agreed to release the first instalment of a six-year, 810 billion yen, low interest package of credits for a number of infrastructure projects and followed up with a 700 billion yen resource development loan in early 1992.

Solicitous handling of Myanmar

Partly for reasons arising out of Japan's long-standing close ties to Myanmar, Tokyo also has been reluctant to follow the lead of the United States and other Western countries in using aid cutoffs as a punishment for repression by the rulers in Yangon. Rather, Japan has used a more subtle mix of aid restrictions and limited concessions to express its disapproval of the regime's failure to respect the results of the May 1990 elections, which were won by pro-democracy opposition groups, and its concern about serious economic and financial mismanagement. In effect, Japan has emerged as a key ally of Myanmar's neighbours in Southeast Asia who prefer a course of "constructive engagement".

Japan joined other donor countries in suspending aid and tying diplomatic recognition of the regime to the holding of free elections in the wake of the September 1988 anti-government agitation against the so-called State Law and Order Restoration Council (SLORC) led by General Saw Maung. Subsequently, however, Japan broke ranks with the West and acted as a G-7 spokesmen for an Asian viewpoint. In early 1989, Japan became the first industrialized country to recognize the Saw Maung regime, and in March 1989 it partially unfroze

Myanmar's aid pipeline to permit work on certain stalled projects. In early 1990, Japan also allowed Myanmar to sell part of its Tokyo embassy property to a Japanese construction company, thereby enabling the impoverished government to reap some US$234 million equivalent in Japanese yen and reportedly triple its hard currency reserves.[85] In late 1990, Japan persuaded Sweden to table for one year a UN resolution that strongly urged the SLORC to cease its human rights abuses and political repression.[86]

Japan has still not relaxed its ban on new aid, although in July 1990 it extended a debt relief loan in the amount of 3.5 billion yen (about US$25 million) to roll over a previous loan repayment in the same amount. In October 1990, the Ministry of Foreign Affairs expressed Japan's increasing concern about the situation in Myanmar and "its strong desire" that the government respect the outcome of the May 1990 election.[87]

Allegedly, the main motivation for Japan's partial reversal of course was commercial. The relaxation of Myanmar's isolation came after thirteen major Japanese companies, including Mitsubishi and Mitsui, formally requested the resumption of diplomatic relations in order to avoid further losses on moribund projects and to counter aggressive poaching by Thai and other regional companies.[88] In addition, Tokyo appears as concerned about economic and financial mismanagement in Myanmar as about political repression. It has used its flexible response policy both to encourage economic reforms and to express disapproval of economic mismanagement.

Although many would argue that Japan missed important opportunities to promote democratization,[89] Japanese policymakers appear to have made a different calculation, one that appears to accept that the current Myanmar authorities cannot climb down from the "tiger" they are riding without being eaten, and that business foregone by Japanese companies — now the most important outside players — will be taken by companies in other Southeast Asian countries that are even less concerned about democracy and human rights. In this respect, Japan appears to be hoping that its policies will, in time, promote the emergence of an alternative power structure more amenable to political liberalization. Meanwhile, it continues to play the role of a sympathetic but stern rich Uncle.

Indochina policy initiatives

Japan's efforts to promote a settlement of the Cambodia conflict have responded primarily to the goals of promoting close co-operation with the ASEAN countries and protecting Tokyo's economic interest in the future development of Indochina. Japan also has felt the need to continue to adhere to the U.S.-led embargo on development aid to Hanoi and Phnom Penh, although its patience with this strategy appears to be wearing thin. Now that the United States has outlined a concrete plan for normalization with Vietnam, Japan stands poised to move quickly to solidify its economic position.

Some see Japan's freezing of aid to Hanoi in 1980 as a reluctant concession to an adverse international environment, not out of any conviction that punishing Vietnam would advance its interests, and Japan has indicated its eagerness to provide large-scale aid to the reconstruction and development of Vietnam and Cambodia once the current conflict is resolved.[89]

In fact, humanitarian assistance contacts and the activities of Japanese trading companies have already moved Japan towards supplanting the Soviet Union as Vietnam's main trading partner, with the exchange of Vietnamese oil, timber, seafood, and scrap iron for Japanese consumer goods and capital equipment. Thus, even with the present limitations on its freedom of action, Japan is increasingly well positioned to bring about the future integration of Indochina into Japan's economic orbit, a development that would add major sources of raw materials, a potentially large market of more than 70 million, and a new pool of cheap labour for offshore manufacturing.[91]

In response to urging from Thailand and other ASEAN countries, Japan agreed to host talks among the rival Cambodian parties in June 1990. In May, the Kaifu government sent Michio Watanabe, former Minister of Finance and a senior Liberal Democratic Party Diet member to Vietnam, China and the United States to lay the groundwork for the negotiations. The most significant result of the Tokyo talks, dubbed a "half success" by Prince Sihanouk, nominal leader of the Cambodian resistance forces, was agreement to divide 12 seats in a proposed Supreme National Council (SNC) between the Phnom Penh government, on the one hand, and the three opposition groups nominally headed by Sihanouk, on the other, instead of four ways, as demanded by the Khmer Rouge. Some see this solution, in retrospect, as advancing the negotiations on the United Nations plan supported by the five permanent Security Council members (Perm-5).[92]

Sihanouk and Prime Minister Hun Sen, head of the Vietnamese-backed Cambodian Government, also signed an accord on the urgent need for restraint to end the conflict and calling for a SNC meeting in July 1990 to establish the modalities of an internal settlement. The restraint agreement had little substantive effect owing to a boycott by the Khmer Rouge. Khieu Samphan, who came to the talks as the Khmer Rouge representative, refused to participate on account of being denied equal status with Sihanouk. The planned follow-up SNC failed to materialize until 1991.

Despite this limited achievement, Japan continued to work quietly towards a solution to the Cambodian conflict. In September 1990, Watanabe made another unofficial trip to Vietnam and Cambodia to press for mutual concessions. Japan has also attempted to use its influence with China to promote rapprochement with Vietnam.

Japan stepped up its efforts again in mid-1991, seemingly to fill the void left by the overthrow of Thai Prime Minister Chatichai, who had led the effort to promote broader international support for the Phnom Penh government. According to some accounts, Tokyo also sought a major foreign policy success to compensate for the "debacle" of its response to the Persian Gulf crisis. In the process, it is said, Japan has entered into a rivalry with Australia, which initiated the current UN peace plan.[93]

Some saw Japan's moves in the first half of 1991 as aimed at accommodating Phnom Penh's concerns that the cease-fire and demobilization of forces provisions under the "Perm-5" UN plan would be exploited by the Khmer Rouge. Japan's initiative, reportedly, provided for step-by-step monitoring of a cease-fire, denying participation in proposed elections to any faction that violates the truce, and the creation of a special body to investigate human rights violations during the period of Khmer Rouge rule.[94] As if to underscore its tacit "tilt" towards Phnom Penh and Hanoi, Japan hosted a visit by Hun Sen in April 1991 for treatment of what is reported as a serious medical condition and talks about a Cambodian settlement.

Economic objectives are widely seen as the main motive force of Japan's initiatives. In the wake of the 1990–91 Persian Gulf crisis, Japan has given indications of heightened interest in developing what may be major oil and gas deposits in Cambodia and off Vietnam's coast. Japan already buys 80 per cent of Vietnam's petroleum exports, amounting to 2.7 million tons in 1990.[95] Japanese oil companies have responded eagerly to invitations from the Cambodian Government to consider undertaking oil exploration based on geophysical data developed earlier by Soviet technicians. According to a representative of the C. Itoh trading company, "the Gulf war taught us again the importance of security [for] our own oil wells."[96] Reportedly, in a visit to Vietnam during 10–14 June 1991, the first such high level visit since 1976, Foreign Minister Taro Nakayama planned to indicate Tokyo's readiness to aid in the development of offshore oil fields in the Tonkin Gulf.[97]

During 1992, Japan stepped up its involvement in the Cambodian situation. In early June 1992, after bitter debate, the Diet passed a limited UN Peace Cooperation bill that will allow Japanese Self-Defense forces to provide logistical support to the UN Transitional Authority in Cambodia (UNTAC), an operation headed by a Japanese diplomat, Yasushi Akashi. In mid-June, the Japanese-sponsored Tokyo Cambodia Aid conference drew unexpectedly high pledges of US$880 million, including US$150–200 million from Japan and US$135 million from the United States. Although doubts remain about whether Japan has any clear plan for dealing with the stalemate over implementation of the UN plan, Tokyo already has asserted itself to an unprecedented degree.

Stepped-up involvement in the Korean peninsula

Japan has also stepped up its diplomatic involvement in the Korean peninsula, primarily in an effort to help stabilize the North-South relationship but also in support of its economic and commercial interests. Japan hosted a visit to Tokyo by South Korean President Roh Tae Woo in June 1990, and the countries held ministerial level talks in Seoul during 26–27 November in preparation for a planned visit by Prime Minister Kaifu in January. Kaifu's visit to Seoul during 9–10 January 1991 itself served to lay the groundwork for Tokyo's normalization talks with North Korea the same month. Reportedly, Kaifu reassured Roh that Japan's negotiations on normalizing relations with North Korea would not undercut Seoul's own efforts to promote better ties, while asking that South Korea show similar sensitivity to Japan's interests as it pursues expanded ties with the Soviet Union.[98]

Thus far these exchanges have produced considerable improvement in the tone of relations, especially as a result of steps by Japan to apologize for its past occupation of Korea and to improve treatment of Korean residents of Japan. They have achieved little substantive progress, however, on underlying economic issues such as South Korean complaints about Japan's large trade surplus and the unwillingness of Japanese firms to be sufficiently forthcoming about sharing technology.[99] Nor do they appear to have completely alleviated each country's concerns about the goals of the other *vis-à-vis* third countries such as North Korea, the Soviet Union and China.

Japan's dialogue with North Korea has moved in fits and starts since the visit of a parliamentary delegation led by Shin Kanemaru to Pyongyang in September 1990. That visit created a stir because of reported offers of future "compensation" which had not been cleared with the Ministry of Foreign Affairs. The parliamentary delegation served as a prelude to official talks in Beijing in October 1990, and precedent setting discussions in Pyongyang in January and May 1991, all to little apparent effect. During the course of this dialogue, new information surfaced about North Korea's apparent nuclear weapons programme, and Tokyo has begun to consider additional measures to deal with what could become a frightening security threat. Partly in response to South Korean urging, Japan pressed North Korea to put its nuclear facilities under international inspection by the International Atomic Energy Agency (IAEA) as a condition for normalization, while North Korea demanded compensation for Japan's colonial rule.[100] Given Japan's strong security interest in taking a hard line on the nuclear issue, the prospects for normalization remain linked to Pyongyang's fulfilment of its January 1992 commitment to open its nuclear facilities to IAEA inspection and other aspects of its recent accord with Seoul.

Stabilizing role in the Philippines

In the Philippines, Japan has continued to maintain an informal partnership with the United States, while cautiously stepping up its own
involvement. As of 1988, Japan provided fully two-thirds of all bilateral
ODA received by Manila, compared to 15 per cent supplied by the
United States.[101] Tokyo is the mainstay of the 19-nation, multi-billion
dollar, Multilateral Aid Initiative (MAI). Reportedly, Japan played a key
role in structuring the MAI, notably by insisting on the participation
of the World Bank as the co-ordinator and by influencing the emphasis
on infrastructure development in support of private business investment
in key sectors of the economy.[102] Official Japanese involvement seems
to be having an effect. While remaining wary of the country's political
instability, Japanese businesses are stepping up their investment in the
Philippines through participation in aid-related infrastructure projects
and commercial ventures with potentially lucrative and quick returns.

Japan's policies towards the Philippines have been designed to under-
pin stability and, indirectly, to support a continued U.S. military presence,
especially at Subic Bay. In the wake of the eruption of Mount Pinatubo,
which caused the abandonment of Clark Air Base, and the vote of the
Philippines Senate to reject the treaty extending the U.S. use of Subic
Bay, Japan faces a dilemma. In all likelihood, U.S. aid to the Philippines will be cut back once its forces withdraw from Subic. In this
event, Japan will likely become the single most important country to
the Philippines — regardless of whether it seeks to become more active
in economic and political support of Manila, or shrinks from seeking
to play a larger role.[103]

Firmer hand in Thailand

Japan has been perhaps the most willing to utilize its leverage in dealing
with Thailand, a country with whom it has a unique, century-long,
history of close cultural and political ties. Tokyo found its deepening
and profitable relationship with Thailand, Japan's "first point of contact
in ASEAN",[104] threatened by the February 1991 coup that overthrew
Prime Minister Chatichai, and it acted with unaccustomed vigour to

protect its interests. Japan froze its aid programme until the military coup leaders released Chatichai from confinement, installed a civilian government and pledged to maintain continuity of economic policy.[105] The bloody suppression of the May 1992 popular uprising against the government of General Suchinda Kraprayoon rattled Tokyo but found the Japanese Government still reluctant to take a stand that might be regarded as interventionist. The crisis, however, accelerated an ongoing re-evaluation of Japan's economic commitment to Thailand.

Continuing avoidance of system-wide responsibility

"Leading from behind" on Asia-Pacific economic co-operation

For reasons that are central to the debate about its potential for leadership, Japan has shown extreme reluctance to assume leadership in the area of its greatest strength. Despite its status as the "core economy" of the Asia-Pacific region, Japan played its cards close to the vest on the issue of regional economic co-operation and avoided a leadership role. Tokyo gave qualified support when Australian Prime Minister Bob Hawke called for the creation of an Asia-Pacific Economic Co-operation entity during a January 1989 speech in Seoul. Subsequently, after insuring that the plan would include the United States and was acceptable to the ASEAN countries, Japan became a major but behind-the-scenes supporter.

Behind Japan's initial reticence lay a power struggle between the Ministry of Foreign Affairs (MFA), which seems to have been taken by surprise by the Hawke speech, and MITI, which strongly favoured the plan and may even have played a role in suggesting it. While MITI was seeking to mobilize support of the Australian proposal in Asian capitals, the foreign ministry appeared more concerned about the potential diplomatic problems raised by the plan, including initial opposition of some ASEAN countries and knotty questions such as how to accommodate the "three Chinas" — the PRC, Hong Kong and Taiwan. For these reasons, the MFA initially appeared to lean towards the existing, unofficial, Pacific Economic Co-operation Conference (PECC) forum.[106]

Although MFA's concerns were substantially alleviated by the outcome of the July 1989 post-ministerial meeting of the Japan-ASEAN dialogue, it reportedly remained in conflict with MITI over "turf" issues that had implications for the domestic power of the rival bureaucracies. These included concerns that MITI would seek a larger economic co-operation role by promoting expanded government-private sector initiatives that would fall under MITI's jurisdiction. As a result of unresolved issues, the MFA and MITI sent rival delegations to the November 1989 Canberra meeting,[107] leading some wits to dub it the "Two Japans' Conference".

Eventually, the struggle appeared to be resolved in favour of MITI, under the rationale that the main business of APEC would be economic co-operation. MFA officials reportedly deferred to the MITI representatives at a follow-up May 1990 senior officials level meeting in Singapore.[108] Japan now is widely perceived as an enthusiastic backer of the APEC concept as a vehicle for checking further trends towards protectionism in North America and Europe, but also is still seen as preferring to "lead from behind".[109]

Beyond the bureaucratic struggles lie deeper sources of Japanese reticence. Both the APEC proposal and Malaysian Prime Minister Mahathir's call for an East Asian Economic Group at a March 1991 conference in Bali tend to force the issues of the balance of power between the United States and Japan, and the degree to which Tokyo is prepared to accept direct responsibility for the health and vitality of the Asia-Pacific region. The latter issue has direct relevance to the continuing inequality of trade ties between Japan and its regional trading partners. Thus far, these appear to be issues that neither the Japanese leadership establishment nor the public are prepared to confront.

Inevitable "pull" effect of Japan's economic power

Although Japan's leaders may shun a strongly assertive regional role, the country's enormous economic power exerts its own "pull" effect, leading Asia-Pacific countries to seek to manipulate the Japanese connection to advance their own objectives. Under Prime Minister Chatichai, Thailand appeared to be counting on Japan as the fulcrum for its aspirations to become the key economic power on mainland Southeast Asia and the window for the redevelopment of Indochina. Kraisak Choonhavan, then head of the Thai advisory team on the Cambodian issue, and son of former Prime Minister Chatichai, was quoted as telling reporters in April 1990 that, "It is time that the Japanese get themselves more involved in regional politics, because times have changed and the world's political equation has changed."[110]

Malaysian Prime Minister Mahathir's efforts to use the Japanese connection for both domestic and international leverage have received mixed reviews in Tokyo and the region itself. Mahathir's attachment to a "Look East" development strategy has deep roots and holds an important place in his world view. According to some reports, the Japanese suspended aid projects in two states — Sabah and Kelantan — that deserted Mahathir's UNMO party in the October 1990 election, pending a reassessment by Kuala Lumpur of its policy towards the dissident areas. While such actions may reflect simple prudence, they illustrate the ways in which the Japanese connection can work to the benefit of those in power.[111]

With regard to his EAEG proposal, there appears to be some gain from the Japanese connection, in this case to counter feared "protectionist" tendencies in the United States. The Malaysian leader and others see negotiations on a North American Free Trade Agreement (NAFTA) as potentially inhibiting Asian access to the U.S. market. Mahathir's EAEG plan stands little chance of acceptance under present circumstances although the ASEAN countries have tepidly endorsed a shadow of it as an East Asian Economic Caucus. It proved an embarrassment to Japan's policymakers, who strongly oppose the idea of an Asian trade grouping that excludes the United States. Regardless of Tokyo's distinct lack of enthusiasm, Mahathir's proposal can be seen as a direct consequence of Japan's emergence as the dominant Asian economy and a regional leader whose global influence may sometimes be turned to the advantage of its weaker neighbours instead of itself. Moreover, despite the awkward issues raised by the Malaysian proposal, it may also be seen by many

in the Japanese power structure as serving to be a useful warning to the
United States that Japan has an Asian card that should not be ignored
as U.S. policymakers consider their NAFTA proposal.

5
Problems and prospects for Japan's influence in Asia

Japan's record suggests that while its ability to translate its economic power into influence increasingly appears unarguable, a number of deeply rooted problems still limit its capacity to exert global or even regional leadership. Among the more prominent are: uncertainties about the purposes of Japanese activism and its ability to lead; internal political weaknesses; cultural and value system gaps between Japan and other Asia-Pacific countries; the inherent limitations of its aid diplomacy and negative attitudes stemming from Tokyo's past effort to militarily dominate the region.

Uncertainty about Japan's goals and ability to lead

To date, Japan's Asia-Pacific foreign policy initiatives have tended to raise doubts about the purposes of Japanese activism rather than confirm Tokyo's status as a bona fide regional leader. Analysts still question whether Japan really has a clear sense of how it wants to use its growing power. Probably most Japanese would still judge their country as "bereft of a sense of direction, and uncertain about the future".[112] A minority view is that "Japan is beginning to show a subtle but powerful leadership",[113] but that a perception gap has opened up in the ways that

Japanese and foreigners see the country. Former Foreign Minister
Dr Saburo Okita wrote in 1989 that "things are changing very abruptly,
and it is important to recognize that Japan is in a transitional phase".[114]
A number of powerful LDP leaders, including Foreign Minister Michio
Watanabe, former Secretary General Ichiro Ozawa, and Prime Minister
Kiichi Miyazawa have taken outspokenly activist positions regarding
Japan's international role.

Lack of credibility of Asia-Pacific political initiatives

Despite its greater activism, Japan's efforts at regional leadership have
not borne much fruit thus far or significantly enhanced Tokyo's credibility. Overall assessments of Kaifu's 1989 South Asian tour were not
flattering. At the time, commentators concluded that the complexities
of regional disputes, and reluctance to appear to take sides, would continue to make Japan more relevant as an aid giver than as a mediator
or leader.[115] Similar scepticism attended Kaifu's May 1991 Southeast
Asian tour, despite his lofty rhetoric. Some press reporting suggested
that the ASEAN countries remained more interested in the prospects
of increased aid from Japan than the benefits of a larger Japanese
political role.[116]

Japan's efforts to promote a Cambodian settlement also earned mixed
reviews, especially from countries that themselves aspired to play a
mediating role. One perspective saw Japanese activism as dubious in
purpose and commitment. In early May 1990, in the wake of Japan's
early efforts to promote a settlement, the *Jakarta Post* questioned
"whether we are now watching the birth of a Thai-Japanese diplomatic
initiative in this region with a concerted approach in Cambodian peace
diplomacy as a curtain raiser" or something less. The paper preferred
to attribute the confusion about Japan's policy to Kaifu's obliqueness
and the problems of simultaneous translation during his Jakarta press
conference, but asked for more transparency in Japan's objectives and
said that "if Japan considers the solution of the Cambodian conflict is
also ultimately beneficial to its wider security interests in the region,

then it should not merely dabble in the Cambodian peace diplomacy half-heartedly".[117]

These kinds of doubts were not put to rest by Japan's re-engagement as a peace broker in 1991. Given the seeming irreconcilable objectives of the Cambodian parties, puzzlement about Japan's objectives was not surprising. Some judged that Japan sought simply to maintain the appearance of momentum while "boosting its growing political role in the region".[118] A less cynical interpretation was that Japan had few illusions about the prospects for reconciliation among the warring Cambodian factions, but that Tokyo foreign policy managers sought to stabilize and perpetuate an evolving sense of *détente* in Southeast Asia even if a real settlement of the Cambodian tangle might require considerable time. From this perspective, Tokyo's new willingness to risk its prestige can be seen as concrete evidence of Japan's aspirations for regional leadership, even if the goals remained modest ones.

Limitations imposed by Japan's political system, culture and values

Japan's political system, culture and related values all constitute major limitations on Japan's ability to turn its economic power into international influence and leadership. Despite increasingly stronger expressions of intent to play a larger role in world affairs, Tokyo's actual ability to play a larger role probably will remain constrained in the foreseeable future. Limiting factors include a continued tendency towards insularity among the general public, the parochial outlook of political faction leaders, a lack of specificity regarding concepts of "responsibility" for global leadership and other internal disagreements about Japan's stance towards the outside world.

Political system limitations

While increasing numbers of officials and academics talk of Japan assuming responsibilities commensurate with its economic power, a strong theme among Western and Japanese analysts is that systemic factors inevitably favour least-common-denominator policies supported by vested economic and bureaucratic interests. Some go so far as to describe the Japanese system as a "truncated pyramid" with no single head, and to assert that Japan is not even a "state" in the accepted meaning of the term.[119] Others argue that Japan is "uncomfortable with the pressure put upon it to act as a global leader", and would rather be No. 2 to the United States than bring various special interests to heel in the service of the global economic system.[120]

Little lustre was added to the image of Japanese leadership by the Recruit scandal, and the fall of Prime Ministers Takeshita and Uno. Prime Minister Kaifu's success in leading the LDP to victory in the February 1990 elections raised his standing somewhat, but ultimately he could not shake off the impression that he was largely a figure-head, and that real decision-making authority lay with powerful LDP faction leaders. The faction leaders proved their dominance in September 1991 when they took him out of the running for the LDP Presidency — and hence a second term as Prime Minister — for having the temerity to push political reform legislation that they opposed.

Bureaucratic infighting

At the level of the permanent bureaucracy, the ambivalence of Japan about its regional political role appears partly a function of competing economic-bureaucratic interests. The range of perspectives includes the Ministry of Foreign Affairs, which tends to protect the U.S.-Japan alliance, take a hard line on Japan–Soviet relations, and seek to promote a benevolent image of Japan to the outside world; MITI, whose close ties to the Tokyo-based business establishment give it a more neo-mercantilist approach to Japan's foreign economic relations; and the Finance Ministry, which also shares MITI's pro-business bias but competes with MITI for bureaucratic turf, and acts as a brake on economic liberalization and on spending for foreign aid and defence.

The tentativeness of Japan's efforts to assume greater political leadership also reflects the more basic realities such as confusion among

Japanese from all walks of life, who feel unsure about their country's role in the world. The Japanese public remains generally supportive of political initiatives aimed at enhancing their country's prestige, but they still find the rest of the world difficult to understand and potentially hostile. Japanese citizens appear to feel little power to influence politics themselves and seem persuaded that Japan's success is fragile, and that the country remains vulnerable to a number of threats ranging from economic collapse to natural disasters.

Both the August 1990 Iraqi invasion of Kuwait and the unsuccessful August 1991 Soviet coup showed the Japanese foreign policymaking apparatus to extremely bad advantage. In the Gulf crisis, Japan's reactions were constantly late and — for an aspiring global leader — inadequate. In the Soviet internal crisis, Prime Minister Kaifu's temporizing stance and "failure to make any decisive remarks" led to scathing criticism by rival LDP leaders and left Japan without any influence over the U.S. and European decision-making process.[121] In both crises, Japanese leaders failed to grasp the significance of the situation and the necessity of adopting a participatory approach regarding the coalescence of international opinion. In contrast with Japan's superior capacity for collecting and acting on commercial intelligence, its political leaders and foreign policy bureaucrats appear to lack an effective intelligence and decision-making system.

Analysis of the Gulf policy failure has tended to focus much of the blame on the Foreign Ministry and what its critics see as its overly rigid bureaucracy. As of mid-1991, a Special Advisory Council on Enforcement of Administrative reform was expected to call for weakening the power of the Gaimusho (MFA) and place more decision-making authority in the hands of the Cabinet Secretariat. In what looked like a typical bureaucratic power play by MFA rivals, the Council was also expected to propose the more extensive appointment of non-MFA personnel to diplomatic posts, the appointment of more non-career diplomats and the creation of a minister without portfolio for foreign policy. The Foreign Ministry counterattacked vigorously, charging that the proposed reforms would only worsen an already chaotic policymaking process, and arguing that "the essential problems lie in the very fundamentals of national policy", which a MFA policy paper reportedly

cited as "the lack of a principle to deal with international conflict of
interest and a lack of strong political leadership".[122]

Negative influence of domestic politics

Domestic politics often complicates or even undercuts the foreign policymaking process. For instance, Shin Kanemaru's visit to North Korea
in his capacity as an LDP official revealed a major gap between the
LDP leadership and the Ministry of Foreign Affairs. Initiatives such
as Kanemaru's promise of financial compensation to North Korea for
Japan's colonial rule in return for agreement on normalization, and
other party-level initiatives regarding Indochina, seem to indicate a
growing encroachment on foreign policymaking by LDP faction leaders.
While this development may at times give a needed shake-up to the
bureaucracy, the underlying attitudes of the party leaders and their
business backers often tend to reflect a cruder and more insensitive
side of Japan's world view whose impact on policy may ultimately
create more friction with its Asian neighbours and the United States.

The selection of Miyazawa as prime minister illustrated two relevant
principles of Japanese politics. First, that factional politics remains the
ultimate arbiter of the leadership selection. Second, that experience in
foreign affairs and the ability to represent Japan to the rest of the world
(not to mention carrying the party to electoral victory) have become
important basic requirements for being regarded as a contender. This
suggests that Japan has a growing potential for assuming greater international leadership but that ultimately this potential will remain hostage
to back-room politics that has little to do with the issues at stake.

Cultural and value system limitations

Despite the eager adoption by many countries of Japanese formulas
for economic success, and the growing spread of Japanese popular
culture, the affinity between the Japanese and their Asia-Pacific neighbours remains low. Asia-Pacific countries tend to believe that Japan

fundamentally does not care very much about them. In survey after survey, Japanese business executives are portrayed as domineering and insensitive to local feeling. This includes a double standard for behaviour at home and abroad. "You don't have to worry about *nemawashi* [consensus-building] over here," a Canon executive was quoted in a March 1991 article on Japanese operations in Malaysia.[123]

These attitudes are also underscored by the still substantially self-serving quality of Japan's aid programmes and the tendency of large Japanese overseas contingents to cluster in colonies and recreate the Japanese way of life. The latter is hardly an unknown expatriate phenomenon, but one that is more accentuated among the Japanese even though they themselves are Asians. In fact, the very "Asianness" of Japan can be an added source of perceived threat due to visceral ethnic feelings that seem to increase with the degree of physical closeness. Considerable evidence suggests that despite Japan's growing involvement in Asia, the Japanese themselves tend to identify more with the West and view other Asian cultures as inferior.

Limitations of aid diplomacy

Japan's programme of aid to Asia, while undoubtedly a major tool of influence and an asset to Japanese business, can also be a negative factor in its relations with Asia-Pacific countries. First, although the impression abounds of unlimited Japanese coffers, resources available to the government are finite and cannot be increased except at the expense of domestic policy objectives. While Japan may have huge trade surpluses, its budget deficit has been relatively larger than that of the United States as a share of total outlays (15.3 per cent for Japan for FY 1988 versus 12.5 per cent for the United States) and its national debt is comparable as a share of GNP (56.6 per cent for Japan versus 55.2 per cent for the United States in FY 1988).[124] Many Japanese, in fact, regard their country as financially weak notwithstanding its high GNP.

The steady increases in the aid budget in the face of cutbacks in domestic programmes have a substantial political cost. Japan is now straining to maintain its longer term commitments to raise its aid levels in absolute terms and as a share of GNP. During 1990, in fact, Japan's aid budget increased by only about 2.8 per cent in dollar terms. It fell behind the United States as a global aid donor, and aid to Asian countries grew only slightly. The 1991 ODA White Paper explicitly acknowledges that new measures to strengthen the national consensus regarding ODA, including public relations and education, will be necessary if Japan is to achieve the target of US$50 billion in ODA for the five-year period ending March 1993 (end of FY 1992). Estimates that future resource transfers increasingly would come from recycling private sector surpluses, rather than government funds,[125] have been called into question by the deepening economic recession and shrinkage of corporate profits.

Of more immediate importance, a log-jam has developed on the dispersal side. Under the current "four ministries" system, each aid loan requires the concurrence of the ministries of foreign affairs, finance, MITI, and the Economic Planning Agency — a system prone to deadlock and occasional political interference from ruling LDP politicians. The implementation problems have been acknowledged frankly in the most recent Ministry of Foreign Affairs report on Japan's ODA.[126]

At the recipient end, Japanese aid is creating some problems in Tokyo's foreign relations. Due to the rapid appreciation of the yen in 1986 and 1987, aid recipients have become hard pressed to keep up their payments on past loans. About 40 per cent of Indonesia's US$51 billion foreign debt is in yen loans, while its main export earner, petroleum, is denominated in dollars. Facing the need to come up with US$7 billion to service its debt in the 1990–91 fiscal year, the Indonesian Government was disappointed when, in the course of his May 1990 visit to Jakarta, Prime Minister Kaifu only promised US$1.8 billion in new aid. The commitment was less than the US$2.1 billion pledged in the previous year.[127]

A number of other Asian aid recipients, including Malaysia, Thailand and the Philippines, face similar loan repayment problems. The request by Asian aid recipients for loans payable in dollars was not met with enthusiasm in Japan. As "an exceptional case", Japan's Export-Import Bank loaned Indonesia US$200 million in U.S. dollars in 1988, repayable over ten years, in addition to authorizing some US$2.3 billion in yen loans a few months earlier. Both the dollar loan and the yen loans were untied, fast-disbursing infrastructure loans.[128]

Aid recipients also perceive that Japanese largesse has its price, and resent efforts to use aid as a lever to secure favoured economic access for Japanese businesses. India reportedly has grumbled about "invisible conditionalities" attached to past loans that compromise its traditional arms-length dealings with multinationals and its nationalistic economic policies. In 1989, New Delhi was said to regard as "too much" Tokyo's demands for reductions in duties on imports from Japan as an ODA quid pro quo.[129] Following Prime Minister Kaifu's April 1990 visit to India, during which he announced a large increase in Japanese aid, the then Indian Prime Minister V.P. Singh made clear that aid would not provide a door-opener to the Indian market.[130] More recently, however, in an alleged quid pro quo for Japanese support of critically needed balance of payments loans from the IMF, India may have yielded to Japanese pressure to reopen bidding on an oil field project which had previously been won by Korean companies. Reportedly, Japanese companies previously had been barred from competing as a result of a "pay-off" scandal involving a consortium headed by the Sumitomo company.[131]

Countries often resent the strong *de facto* tied aspect of certain kinds of Japanese aid, and the growing dominance of Japanese construction firms in Japanese-aided projects. In 1987, Japanese Prime Minister Nakasone had to cancel his planned inauguration of a Japanese-funded historical study centre in Thailand's ancient capital of Ayutthaya, due to the Thai Government's objections to the failure to involve Thai consultants and contractors, and criticism of its inappropriate architecture.[132] More recent reports suggest that these problems have continued in Thai-Japan aid relations, especially the dominance of Japanese contractors in bidding for Japanese-funded construction projects.[133]

Despite these strains, Japanese aid funds are eagerly sought, and are key to local leaders' ambitions for promoting growth and development. The continuing sources of friction, however, underscore the still highly commercial-oriented and competitive aspects of Japan's aid diplomacy as well as the inability of Japan's foreign and economic policy managers to make hard decisions that involve taking a broader view of the country's interests, or to put Japanese prestige on the line in the interest of regional leadership.

Conflicting objectives of economic co-operation

A more serious, long-term problem is a substantial degree of mismatch in the basic objectives of economic co-operation as viewed by Japan and its Asia-Pacific neighbours. While Japanese aid and investment is sought by countries eager to industrialize, the participants in co-operative ventures often have very different notions of the desired outcome. This is especially true for concepts of the appropriate "division of labour". While Japan's business leaders and economic managers are content to shift certain industries and product lines towards the NIEs, those countries are not willing to produce only intermediate goods. Especially in the face of rising costs and currency appreciation, the NIEs must increasingly challenge Japan's higher technology industries in order to maintain their export growth.

Likewise, China, the ASEAN countries and other developing nations are eager to become new NIEs, not simply low wage locations for Japanese offshore production or buyers of Japanese technology. Despite their conversion to economic liberalization, most of the Asian countries and their political leaders remain doggedly autarchic in outlook. Whereas Japanese companies seek to regionalize production according to each country's endowments and transfer the minimum technology necessary, host countries still prefer balanced industrialization and the maximum technology transfer.

A classic example of this conflict of goals can be seen in the efforts of Malaysia's state-owned Perusahaan Otomobil Nasional (Proton) company's joint venture with Mitsubishi Motor Corporation to build the national car, the Proton Saga. In this case, Malaysia's desire to build a national car with maximum local content conflicted with Mitsubishi's goal of getting a foothold in the Southeast Asian market and regionalizing production operations on a multi-country basis. Most of the costs and risks were borne by the Malaysian company, while Mitsubishi gained exports of equipment and parts, consultancy contracts, and ultimately, management of the enterprise.

At present, the project is seen as a success by the Malaysian Government, and it is touted in the press as evidence of the success of Mahathir's development strategy. The success mainly arises out the willingness of the Japanese partners to indulge — for a steep price — Mahathir's national car aspirations. However, beneath the superficial success of rising production and even exports to the United Kingdom lie huge costs related to uneconomic production, tax breaks and massive, government-backed debts.[134] From the perspective of Japanese officials, the involvement of Mitsubishi in the project has achieved exactly the results hoped for, making Japanese business "an integral part of one of the world's fastest growing economies, with minimal risk".[135]

Negative feelings towards Japan

Both the past and the present continue to generate negative feelings about Japan in the Asia-Pacific region, although to date these attitudes have neither been overwhelming nor disabling handicaps to the expansion of Japanese influence. Unlike the widespread anti-Japanese demonstrations that greeted Prime Minister Tanaka during a tour of Southeast Asia in 1974, Japan's recent heavy and obvious economic presence in Asia has not thus far led to any significant outburst of anti-Japanese sentiment save for anti-Japanese Chinese student demonstrations in late 1985. This in itself speaks volumes about how much Asian attitudes about development, especially the role of the private sector, have changed in the past 15 years. On the other hand, the situation could change quickly should growth falter, urban–rural income disparities become too pronounced, or Japanese economic dominance become too apparent.

While ruling parties and political leaders in a number of Asian countries have become heavily dependent on Japan's economic role to insure their own political prospects, most leaders worry about overdependence on Japan. Singapore's former Prime Minister Lee Kuan Yew probably echoed the sentiments of most Asian leaders when he told

European leaders at the World Economic Forum at Davos, Switzerland, that the NIEs welcomed European co-operation "because they are keen on an economic order in Asia that is not dominated by Japan".[136] Lee and other Southeast Asian leaders have expressed anxiety about being "left alone" in the region with a dominant Japan.

Asian countries tend to see the operations of Japanese firms as setting them apart from other foreign economic collaborators. While Japanese businesses have a good reputation for fulfilling agreements once a bargain is struck, governments and potential business partners often criticize Japanese tactics in the stage leading up to a collaboration or investment decision. Local firms resent exclusivist business relationships and complain about the reluctance of Japanese investors to employ local managers, procure supplies and components from local companies, or provide significant technology transfer.[137]

Notwithstanding Prime Minister Mahathir's active promotion of the Japanese connection, friction between Malaysians and Japanese investors appears higher than in other countries. As in the case of the Proton project, Malaysians often chafe at their dependence on Japan. The head of a national "social awareness society" — Aliran — put it bluntly in a March 1991 article in the *Far Eastern Economic Review*, "Japan sets the agenda for industrialization in Southeast Asia . . . This is the nature of economies that are dependent and economies that are in a position to dictate."[138]

Japanese businessmen and tourists are now as ubiquitous in Asia as Japanese exports. The hotel and retail sales industries in Singapore, Hong Kong and other Asian marketing centres are highly geared to catering to Japanese tourists, with department stores advertising door-to-door delivery anywhere in Japan. With lots of spending power but little knowledge of the local scene, Japanese businessmen and tourists are often seen as haughty and demanding. The display of anti-Japanese bumper stickers in Taiwan and popular songs about the "Samurai" buying up land in Thailand[139] attest to significant image problems arising out of the growing Japanese presence.

Occasional signs of overt resentment suggest the potential for a serious reaction should Japan misstep in the bilateral political arena. Chinese student demonstrations in late 1985 responded to a perceived revival of Japanese militarism and "economic aggression" in the form of a soaring bilateral trade deficit.[140] Remarks by the Japanese education minister in 1986 that glossed over Japan's World War II role in Korea and China led to calls for a public apology from South Korea and necessitated a hasty fence-mending trip to Beijing by Prime Minister Nakasone.[141]

In Australia, anti-Japanese feeling often is just beneath the surface and occasionally overt, especially among the older generation. A Japanese-proposed "city of the future", a multifunction and multinational urban centre for industry, research, education and leisure, sparked intense controversy during the April 1990 national election, which was narrowly won by the Labour Party. Liberal Party criticism of the plan provoked Prime Minister Bob Hawke to warn against "insulting" the Japanese and other Asians. Widespread public opposition to the plan is seen as indicative of "ambivalence" towards Japan, at best, and "paranoia about Japan trying to take control of Australia by economic means", at worst.[142]

The Japanese are moving slowly to address some of these problems. In anticipation of South Korean Roh Tae Woo's May 1990 trip to Japan, the Japanese Government partially regularized the status of about 680,000 third and later generation ethnic Koreans by ending a requirement to be fingerprinted and easing travel restrictions. The South Korean president also insisted on a public apology from the new Emperor, Akihito, for Japan's past aggression against Korea. While the oblique form of the apology did not fully satisfy South Korean public opinion, Prime Minister Kaifu himself was more specific in his apology. Overall assessments of the trip were positive, but a subsequent January 1992 visit by Prime Minister Miyazawa was marred by new controversy over the forced recruitment of Korean "comfort women" during World War II and other criticisms of Japan.

Japan has increased its sensitivity to Asian opinion in direct proportion to its rising presence and diplomatic activism. The Kaifu government went to great lengths to reassure Chinese, Korean and Southeast Asian opinion regarding the spring 1991 deployment of its minesweepers to the Persian Gulf. The ships transitted regional waters during Kaifu's April–May 1991 Southeast Asian tour, during which time he made his "sincere contrition" for the harm caused by Japan in World War II the centrepiece of his message to the ASEAN countries.[143]

In spite of this progress towards reducing the burden of history, most Asian countries still regard Japan as not having adequately come to terms with its past. In advance of Roh's trip to Japan, the *Straits Times* of Singapore observed that while other past victims of Japanese aggression "may display less overt anti-Japanese feelings than the Koreans, the fact remains that suspicions about the Japanese still run very deep in most of Asia" and that after 45 years "something is obviously wrong in the state of Japanese relations with its neighbours".[144] Press reportage on Kaifu's 1991 ASEAN tour suggested that Singapore's Prime Minister Goh Chok Tong and other regional leaders were "apprehensive" about how Japan would employ its economic power in the region and were still not completely confident about Japan's intentions.[145]

Even its apologies tendered to China and Korea have been extracted only under pressure, and then couched in terms of "regret" rather than guilt. Moreover, the Japanese remain ambiguous about the apology process, at best. During 1991, the Education Ministry reportedly provided guidance for the most recent social science textbooks that was more nationalistic than in the past, and toned down references to issues such as the "Rape of Nanking".[146]

During his September 1991 tour of Southeast Asia, Emperor Akihito vowed that Japan would never again unleash "the horrors" of what he called "that unfortunate war", but didn't make an apology, as such. This was explained as partly owing to the fact that "Thailand, Indonesia and Malaysia are less eager for apologies than China and South Korea". Other factors reportedly included a desire not to involve the new Emperor too deeply in unpopular actions. Press accounts noted that a kind of backlash has emerged in Japan because "many Japanese say they are weary of being asked to apologize for something that ended long before they were born".[147]

Some of these problems are inherent in any unequal economic and political relationship, and bear kinship to past "Yankee go home" reactions against American influence in parts of Asia and elsewhere. Past and current instances of anti-Japanese feeling raise the possibility that, in the future, Japan could face a nationalistic reaction to its highly visible presence and could be blamed if rapid growth creates destabilizing social fissures.

The factors that work to limit Japan's influence do not, on balance, appear incapacitating. Japan's attractiveness as an economic success model remains strong. Although the impact of Western democratic ideas and popular culture continues to spread, the Japanese formula for development tends to have far more relevance in the minds of most Asian political élites than the Western model. The expansion into the region of Japanese industry has already made major changes in the work cultures of Asian economics. In their efforts to make themselves congenial places for Japanese investment, a number of Asian countries has achieved unprecedented progress in the development of their economic infrastructure, even as they fight a seemingly losing battle against the ills of rapid industrialization — pollution, traffic congestion and rampant urban population growth.

For the moment, the appeal of Japanese aid and investment, and the potential size of the Japanese market, seems more important than negative feelings against Japan. The leaders of other Asian countries are acquiring a vested interest in the benefits of the Japanese connection. Countries like Thailand, which enjoyed investment-fuelled double digit growth until a slight downturn in 1989, and Malaysia, whose exports have grown at a double-digit rate following the establishment of Japanese offshore production facilities, are not looking too hard for the downside of Japan's expanding economic role. Leaders such as Mahathir in Malaysia derive positive political benefits from ventures such as the Proton car, regardless of the arguable value of the project to the national economy.[148]

Attitudes towards a larger Japanese regional security role are another matter entirely. Some countries may find it expedient to encourage Japan as a future counterweight to China or as a stabilizing power following a U.S. withdrawal from the region. Many more, with lasting memories of Japan's World War II role, remain actively fearful of any hint of a militarily resurgent Japan.

6
Prospects for a
larger Japanese military role

While Japan's growing political activism has not been matched by any commensurate desire to play a larger regional security role, circumstances are bringing Japanese leaders face-to-face with a need either to revalidate or redefine the country's security posture. Basic issues for Japan include how to adjust to the collapse of Communism in the former U.S.S.R. and the related end of the Cold War, and the likelihood of a substantial reduction in the U.S. military role in the region. Additionally, in the face of a rapid erosion of the lines between civilian and military technology and heightened "technonationalism" in both the United States and Japan, the government must decide where to strike the balance between autonomy and co-operation with the United States in the production of major weapons systems. In dealing with these issues, Japanese policymakers will have to consider both domestic and international opposition to any indication of revived militarism.

The Iraqi invasion of Kuwait and the launching of Operation Desert Storm by the U.S.-led multinational forces greatly hastened this process, and provoked a major political crisis whose effects have not yet played themselves out. Amidst the tumult surrounding the Gulf crisis, there can be discerned a symbolic but significant gain for those who would bring Japan into the ranks of "normal" countries and legitimize the participation of its self-defence forces in internationally sanctioned peace-keeping activities.

Looking around Japan's perimeter, Tokyo's policymakers see a rapidly changing security situation. The Soviet threat is widely perceived as ended, kept alive in the public's mind principally by the continuing dispute over Moscow's retention of the Northern Territories, four northern islands seized from Japan at the end of World War II. Many judge that a settlement or shelving of this dispute — now seen as more likely as a consequence of the prostrate state of the Russian economy and central authority — would greatly enhance Japanese security. Others are not so sure that a resolution of the dispute is likely in the foreseeable future, owing to the considerable strategic importance of the islands and adjacent waters, on the one hand, and a lack of Japanese business enthusiasm for investment in the troubled Russian economy, on the other. Moreover, some judge that a settlement would not necessarily be wholly to the benefit of Japanese security interests, since it would tend to further undercut domestic support for the U.S.-Japan alliance, which remains the fundamental basis of Japanese defence policy.[149]

Although the Soviet threat may have waned, Japanese policymakers find cause for unease in the rest of their neighbourhood. Sources of concern include the uneasy balance of power on the Korean peninsula and increasing evidence that North Korea is working hard to acquire a nuclear weapons capability. China, depending on how its leadership transition develops, could also become a potential threat to Japan's economic interests in the region, if not a physical threat to the Japanese islands. Likewise, the lifting of the Cold War overlay in Southeast Asia may ultimately contribute to greater stability, but could just as easily lead to new conflict situations. In the Philippines, the possibility of intensified civil strife remains.

Meanwhile, several developments such as the September 1991 announcement that short-range ground and sea-based nuclear weapons would be withdrawn from the region, the apparent eviction of U.S. forces from the Philippines and other indicators of a reduced U.S. military role in Asia also raise questions about Japan's future security. New demands by Washington that Tokyo assume most of the costs of basing U.S. forces in Japan, and a stiffening U.S. posture on trade and technology transfer issues have prompted a still small, but increasingly vocal, minority to call for an independent Japanese military posture.

94   *Japan, the U.S., and the Asia-Pacific century*

The more common reaction, typified by the statements of Prime Minister Miyazawa and other leaders, is to underscore in the strongest possible terms that the U.S.-Japan alliance must remain the centrepiece of Japan's foreign and security policy.

The most recent Defense Agency White Paper, issued in 1991, judged that the region surrounding Japan remained "unstable and fluid". This situation, the report said, required a continued defence buildup in line with the 1976 National Defense Program Outline, support for United Nations activities aimed at promoting peace, and continuing close security co-operation with the United States.[150] The White Paper projected a 6.1 per cent increase (yen basis) in the defence budget for FY 1990, the highest growth rate since 1986.[151] Subsequent pronouncements have cautiously welcomed favourable international developments but declared any significant changes in the current defence programme premature.

New directions in defence policy?

The 1990–91 Persian Gulf crisis appears to have precipitated a re-examination of the premises of Japanese defence policy, and laid the groundwork for further loosening the constraints of the "peace constitution" and broadening the scope of self-defence. LDP strategists, with support in the Defense Agency, appear to be crafting a new approach that could take Japan closer in the future to participating in collective security relationships. At present, only security co-operation with the United States is judged constitutionally permissible.

The apparent movement towards concepts of collective security is an outgrowth of the debate over U.S. demands, in the weeks following Iraq's invasion of Kuwait, that Japan establish a physical presence in the Gulf. The Kaifu government's proposal to have unarmed self-defence forces participate in a United Nations Peace Cooperation Force received a cold response in parliament. Not only did the plan meet with opposition from the Socialists and other opposition parties, but it split the LDP itself. Internationalists such as the then LDP Secretary-General Ichiro Ozawa, Kaifu rival and faction leader Michio Watanabe, and

Figure 6.1
Military deployments in and around Japan

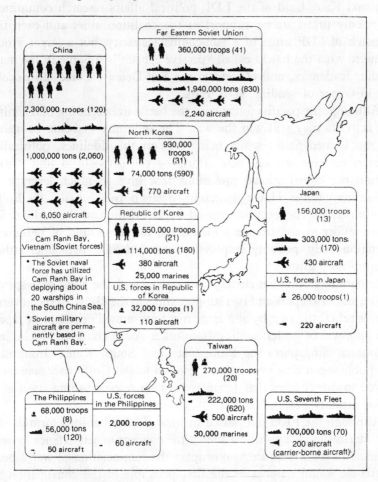

NOTES: 1. Data available from "Military Balance 1989–1990" and other (figures for Japan show actual strength as of the end of fiscal 1989) [sic].
2. The number of U.S. forces personnel stationed in various countries is the total of army personnel and marines.
3. Soviet forces at Cam Ranh Bay are a part of the Soviet forces in the Far East.
4. Combat aircraft in the Far Eastern Soviet Union, China and those maintained by U.S. forces stationed in various countries include naval and marine aircraft.
5. Figures in the parentheses indicate the number of army divisions or vessels.

SOURCES: Notes and figure were reproduced from *Defense of Japan 1990*, Defense Agency, Japan, translated by the *Japan Times*, p. 35.

Mutsuki Kato, head of the LDP political affairs research committee, reportedly urged strong support of the coalition allies and even the dispatch of SDF units in a non-combat capacity, but a larger group clung to what the hawks called "passive egoism".[152] Some in the mass media, academics, and officers of the Self-Defense Forces also spoke out in favour of sending SDF units.

Although the pacifist forces won the battle over sending SDF units, the activists may still win the war. The indignity of being badgered by the United States while being left on the sidelines, politically, appears to have sparked new efforts by the activists to find a way around the constitutional provisions that give so much leverage to anti-military forces. Having gotten its fingers burned initially, the Kaifu government in the post-war period began to prepare the ground for a new effort to construct a legal regime for some kind of peace co-operation body, possibly employing seconded SDF personnel rather than military units.[153]

Important ground has already been broken with the post-war despatch of four minesweepers and two support ships to the Gulf. To the government's relief, the step by and large met with muted criticism in Japan and approval or understanding from other Asian countries, including Indonesia, Singapore, the Philippines and South Korea. Ironically, the public agonizing over how to respond to the Gulf crisis may have served to dispel fears that Japan is bent on re-establishing itself as a major military power.[154]

Although the PKO bill passed in June 1992 is hardly a formula for remilitarization, it appears to stretch the concept of self-defence to new limits. Present trends are to downplay the renunciation of war aspect of Article 9 and emphasize the first principle of the constitution of promoting international peace. Then Prime Minister Kaifu and other leaders have explicitly reminded the Japanese that in addition to forbidding external military involvements or collective security pacts (apart from the U.S.-Japan Security Treaty), the constitution also commits Japan to supporting peace under the United Nations. Conceivably, this change of emphasis could eventually be extended to justify active defence co-operation in the interests of other internationally sanctioned peace efforts or collective defence initiatives presently deemed unconstitutional.

Budget and forces trends

Most predictions of a remilitarized Japan rely on a projection of current trends in Japan's defence budget, the obvious defence potential of Japanese industry and evidence of growing strains in the U.S.-Japan relationship. The Japanese defence budget grew by 6.5 per cent per year during the 1980s, but total defence spending still absorbs only about one per cent of GNP. At US$30.6 billion for FY 1990, Japan's defence budget was still only one-tenth that of the United States.

Beginning in the mid-1970s, Japan initiated a significant buildup of its self-defence capability. The National Defence Program Outline adopted in 1976 and its subsequent revisions up through the 1986–90 Mid-Term Defense Program established specific force level goals. The 1986–90 plan set objectives of acquiring 12 squadrons of modernized fighter aircraft (including eight squadrons of F-15s), 62 naval destroyers and frigates, 16 attack submarines and 100 P-3C anti-submarine surveillance aircraft. These force level objectives, which are somewhat less than those urged by the United States, have now substantially been achieved.[155]

While its military buildup remains highly oriented towards a defensive posture and close co-operation with U.S. forces, these improvements have made Japan a significant regional military power. The Japanese navy, though lacking a power projection capability, is the world's fifth largest and now deploys more destroyers and P-3C anti-submarine aircraft than the U.S. Seventh Fleet. It constitutes a potent military force when compared to the limited blue water capabilities of other Asian navies. Future modernization plans include the joint U.S.-Japanese FSX maritime fighter project and the acquisition of a second escort ship equipped with the AEGIS missile system. These systems will provide qualitative enhancements of Japan's air and maritime defence capabilities while also raising the level of Japan's defence technology and expanding its defence industrial base.

Japan's long-term defence spending plans have been further called into question by the September 1991 announcement of the Bush Administration of its decision to withdraw ground-launched tactical nuclear weapons from the Korean peninsula and to remove most nuclear weapons from the ships of the Seventh Fleet, based in Japan. Japanese leaders have welcomed these steps but have thus far withheld judgment about the implications for Japan's defence posture. Prime Minister Kaifu indicated that Japan would review its defence buildup with a view towards reductions if the U.S. initiative had a positive influence on its security situation.[156]

Technological dimension of Japan's defence capabilities

Some like Steven K. Vogel argue that Japan already has become "a military power in the sense that it has the ability to tip the global balance of power — in either direction".[157] Vogel and other Western analysts have argued that in a variety of ways, Japan's leaders have an increasing ability to use the country's "technological power to promote national security interests".[158] Former U.S. Secretary of Defense Harold Brown has pointed to a possible future involving "Japan's rise to parity or even dominance in various categories of advanced technology, which determine not only economic but also military directions for the balance of this century and beyond".[159] A similar point was made in a more provocative way by a popular Japanese politician, Shintaro Ishihara, who earned instant celebrity status in the United States by arguing that Japan could tip the strategic balance by selling computer microchips to the Soviet Union and withholding them from the United States.[160]

While Ishihara's views are not mainstream ones, "technonationalism" is a strong and growing force in Japan. Increasingly, the Japanese perceive advanced technology as neither specifically "military" nor "civilian" but in varying shades of grey. In the past, the pursuit of *kokusanka*, or "production self-sufficiency", was justified on the basis of gaining production experience in high value-added industries such as electronics and aerospace, reducing costs, gaining knowledge that would enhance Japan's civilian competitiveness, and reaping the benefits of technology "spin-offs". More recently, as a result of the narrowing boundaries between military and civilian technology, Japanese companies and MITI have emphasized the benefits of "spin-on" applications of defence research and development for civilian industry.[161]

Some students of Japanese defence industrial policy, including Michael Green of the Johns Hopkins School of Advanced International Studies (SAIS), see the FSX issue as having provoked an intense policy debate within Japan over the best strategy to maximize the country's economic, technological and foreign policy objectives. Although MITI once promoted defence autonomy or licence production, Green maintains that it concluded in the mid-1980s that "joint development now offered Japanese industry its best entry into the world aircraft market". The Foreign Ministry, Japan Defense Agency (JDA), and the LDP defence *zoku* (caucus of defence-oriented politicians, bureaucrats and industry leaders) also supported this approach in the interest of protecting U.S.-Japan political ties, and in opposition to the autonomist aspirations of the main defence contractors and the Air Self Defense Force (ASDF).[162]

The most significant fact about this debate may not be the particular technonationalist strategy adopted by Japan, but the underlying consensus about the importance of defence industry and defence research and development (R&D) to Japan's future security and competitiveness. Japanese industry, represented by the Keidanren and specific defence producers, is now ranged solidly behind the long term drive for greater defence autonomy, even if in the shorter term this requires joint development with U.S. industry or even the use of American technology when U.S. industry has a competitive edge.[163]

Asian security initiatives

Although Japan has firmly eschewed interest in an overseas military role, a case can be made from reading between the lines that Tokyo has longer term concerns that could involve precisely such a role. Some have argued that "it is only a matter of time before Japan's economic interests will require a Japanese security presence in Asia", and that "stripped of diplomatic frills, recent Japanese remarks about their policy towards the region suggest a remarkably similar geopolitical equation to that prevailing before the Pacific War".[164]

In quiet ways, Japan has already taken steps towards low level security co-operation. Japan already takes a limited number of Asian officers into its military training academies, and in 1991 for the first time since World War II it took two South Korean officers.[165] Reportedly Japan has begun indirectly to underwrite some Asian military projects with its aid programme, including an Indonesian naval base at Teluk Ratai in southern Sumatra and an air defence radar station on the northern part of the same island.[166] The Japanese press has also reported on negotiations with South Korea about air defence co-ordination under the rationale of avoiding unnecessary fighter scrambles over the Tsushima Strait.[167]

A number of Japanese politicians, ex-diplomats and academics have called for talks on forming Asia-Pacific collective security arrangements or an institutionalized dialogue along the lines of the Conference on Security and Cooperation in Europe (CSCE).[168] Given the Japanese pattern of building a national consensus, these indicators deserve to be taken seriously.

Foreign Minister Taro Nakayama created consternation in Kuala Lumpur at the ministerial meeting of the ASEAN countries and their seven dialogue partners when he proposed the establishment of a forum for annual discussions on Asia-Pacific regional security issues. Nakayama's initiative reportedly stemmed from Tokyo's concern that after Prime Minister Kaifu's visit in May "some ASEAN leaders lacked a common understanding with Japan on security issues". This conclusion was said to follow from the apparently unexpected decision of the Philippines in June to recognize North Korea. This action, which partially undercut Japanese efforts to tie recognition to Pyongyang's acceptance of international safeguards and inspection of its nuclear facilities, reportedly "was a signal to Tokyo ... that it must fine-tune security policies with its Asia-Pacific neighbours, especially on sensitive issues such as relations with North Korea".[169]

Nakayama's proposal met with an ambiguous response. Reportedly, the Indonesian Foreign Minister, Ali Alatas, responded that ASEAN could not form such a group because "people will have the wrong impression". The Malaysian and Filipino foreign ministers, Abdullah Ahmad Badawi and Raul Manglapus, both declared that the proposal needed "further study", the classic Japanese formula for rejection. Secretary of State James A. Baker also expressed hesitancy about replacing existing co-operation arrangements "unless we are absolutely certain [that] something else is better".[170]

Somewhat out of character with post-war behaviour, Japanese officials did not beat a hasty retreat in the face of apparent rejection. The Australian Foreign Minister, Gareth Evans, reportedly judged that the ASEAN countries actually meant yes, when they said no.[171] Whether or not the Japanese drew the same conclusion, most indications suggested a growing determination to play a more active security-related role in the region, and of being "less shy of this role".[172] These include the previous port calls of Japan's minesweepers on the way to the Gulf, the likelihood of major participation in any UN peacekeeping operation in Cambodia and a broader determination "not to be the odd man out in the new world order".[173] At the same time, Japan still gives every indication of avoiding a military presence and of doing its utmost to keep the United States actively involved — while continuing to urge that the post-ministerial conferences of the ASEAN countries and their dialogue partners become a forum for regional diplomatic and security discussions.

Dilemmas for regional states

Although China and other Asian countries have objected vocally to any indications of an expanded Japanese military role, a number of signs indicate that some countries in the Asia-Pacific region are already beginning to see some form of a future Japanese regional military presence as inevitable, and are contemplating how to shape that role to their own advantage or counter it.[174] Former Thai Prime Minister Chatichai Choonhavan stirred controversy in May 1990 by reportedly proposing joint naval exercises with Japan in the event of a U.S. withdrawal from the Philippines. The uproar appeared to be fuelled by a positive interpretation that Thai officials gave to the response of the Director of Japan's Self-Defense Agency, whose reported comment that the idea deserved "study" probably should have been read as a polite rejection. Although he later claimed to have been misunderstood,

Chatichai's alleged suggestion provoked sharp rejoinders from the English language daily, *The Nation*,[175] and subsequently from the press and the heads of strategic studies institutes in Malaysia, Indonesia and Thailand.

As noted above, some observers have deemed the ASEAN response to the proposal for a regional security forum as "ambiguous", which in itself suggests at least a partial shift of opinion. One interpretation is that the importance of Japan to the ASEAN countries' economies demanded politeness. Additionally, however, the countries of the region have reason to generally applaud a number of Japan's security-related policies, including its handling of China, the former U.S.S.R. and North Korea, and its supportive role on the Cambodia question. This suggests that while opposition to a direct Japanese military role remains strong, the regional states realize that an evolving power shift in the region may make it necessary to come to terms with a larger Japanese role.[176]

Canberra has also begun to rethink how it can best promote its security interests in the event of a major U.S. withdrawal from the region. These concerns are reflected in the new emphasis on self-reliance as a national policy objective outlined in a 1987 Defence White Paper, and in subsequent official reviews of defence and foreign policy. An official December 1989 review observed that "certainly it would not be useful to assume that the United States will continue to maintain its present level of security interest and activity in this part of the world". The same document took note of Japan's expanding economic role in the region and its more active political role. While the Australian Government expected U.S.-Japan ties to remain close, the document noted that in the event of a breakdown "the repercussions for South East Asia and the South Pacific would be major".[177]

Future posture uncertain

A major question for the future is whether Japan will substantially reduce its high dependence on U.S. security guarantees and/or adopt an independent military posture. Ultimately, the policies of the United States, not Japan's, may be the main variable. Moreover, even Japanese officials who support the current U.S.-Japan security relationship note that the imbalance between Japan's economic power and its military capability has no historical precedent. To date, official policy has been to revalidate both a residual Russian military threat and the rationale for U.S.-Japan security co-operation. Japan continues to regard the acquisition of overt power projection forces as against the constitution, and if anything it has moved recently to reaffirm its commitment to the U.S.-Japan alliance by agreeing to cover most base support costs of U.S. forces in Japan. Given its technological leadership, industrial might and thus far steady adherence to increasing defence budgets, Japan has already lifted itself well above the military capabilities of every power in the region except the former U.S.S.R. and China.

While on balance the current perception of a declining Russian threat would appear to favour anti-military sentiment, the reality is not so clear. On the one hand, the Japan Socialist Party, which has a long pacifist tradition, still controls the upper house of parliament despite having lost credibility in recent months. Public opinion polls continue to reflect anti-military sentiment, and self-defence forces recruitment suffers from the continuing low prestige of military service. Japan's geographic position makes it highly vulnerable to nuclear attack and to the cutting of its trade links in a conventional war. On the other hand, as noted above, awareness is growing — or being promoted — of a range of potential military threats to Japan's interests in the wake of the lifting of the Cold War overlay. Sentiment within the LDP and to a certain extent among the public appears to be leaning towards making Japan a "normal" power by further legitimizing the role of the self-defence forces.

Most evidence still points to modest growth in Japan's military capability, and a slow enhancement of Tokyo's military role in the region. In January 1990, Prime Minister Kaifu contradicted a prediction by French President Mitterrand that Japan would become a major military power. He insisted that Japan would adhere to a strictly defensive posture while maintaining "adequate" forces, and that Tokyo's adherence to the U.S.-Japan Security Treaty was "unshakable". Significantly, however, Kaifu also asserted that Japan's defence policy "ensures not only the defence of our country but also contributes to peace and stability in the East Asian region".[178]

7
Alternative scenarios for the future

Despite the rapid growth of Japan's economic role and influence, the exact shape of future economic, political and security relationships in Asia and the Western Pacific remains uncertain. Conflicting and incomplete data appear to support three different scenarios for Japan's role, and for the structure of regional economic, political and military ties during the next decade. These scenarios parallel, to a certain extent, other efforts at scenario building,[179] but differ in their degree of emphasis on economics as the driving factor, and their focus on Asia and the Western side of the Pacific, rather than the Pacific rim.

Three possible alternative futures are discussed below, along with the conditions that would tend to favour their development. Other possibilities certainly could be imagined, but these are intended to be representative of the broad alternative futures that could follow from Japan's growing economic role and influence in the region.

Assumptions and variables

All of the scenarios involve a mix of factors, including actions by Japan and the United States and exogenous factors such as the prevailing global political and economic situation. An important underlying premise in all of the scenarios is that the current widespread perception of a reduced military threat from the former U.S.S.R. will continue into the foreseeable future and that Russia will remain for a long time a relatively negligible economic actor in Asia. The possibility of a Japan-Russian rapprochement is within the parameters of the scenarios.

Due to its presently clouded political future, China is treated generally as a constant even though it has the potential to make an important difference in the nature of intra-regional economic ties and the regional power balance. Under different assumptions, China has the potential to be (1) a quiet backwater with modest impact on economic and political patterns, as at present; (2) a dynamic new low cost producer and expanding market; or (3) a highly negative disrupter of regional stability. Looking towards 1997, China's policies will strongly influence Hong Kong's role also. Likewise, the evolution of PRC-Taiwan relations could have enormous impact on the future political economy of the Asia-Pacific region.

Another major uncertainty is whether the global economy will continue to grow, and whether current structural problems such as the large U.S. trade deficit can be corrected without a major slowdown in world growth. Unlike the roles of the former U.S.S.R. and China, this factor is incorporated into the scenarios as an active variable.

Conceptual framework

The ultimate impact of the trends discussed above would appear to depend on the future character of U.S. and Japanese interaction with the other Pacific countries and, equally important, with each other. Few dispute the fact that in Asia, the United States and Japan are the countries whose policies and actions are most important at the moment, and that for better or worse Tokyo and Washington are currently linked in a complex relationship of interdependency.

Policy analysts tend to divide over the question of what factors will predominate in the Asian political system of the future. Put in its most simple form, the debate hinges on whether international politics determines economic relationships or vice versa.[180] One currently popular argument is that the very nature of power relationships among states is changing in a direction that gives much more importance to economic power than in the past, a development favouring Japan. The reasons for this shift are diverse and often not clearly articulated, but in general they are tied to the breakdown of the previous intense ideological struggle between East and West and the increasing economic integration of the world along free-market lines.

A variant of this argument is that the relative decline of U.S. manufacturing and financial power, and the even more serious economic crisis facing the former U.S.S.R., also will hasten the evolution of a multi-polar power system. The most popular articulation of such a system features Japan — at least until China realizes its full potential — as the dominant Asian power.

Another approach argues that the calculus of international power remains much as it has been since the emergence of nation states, and that Japan has basic liabilities that militate against world power status, including insufficient raw materials, energy resources, and land mass (for military defence), and a political culture and ideology ill-suited to a world leadership role. Further, some argue that Tokyo's current economic pre-eminence may prove ephemeral in the face of rising "new Japans" like South Korea and Taiwan, or more likely, China's emergence as a true superpower in the next century.

One of the most forceful advocates of this view of continuing U.S. predominance postulates that despite some adverse economic trends, the United States still retains the unique ability to determine the *structure* of "the global political economy within which other states, their political institutions, economic enterprises and (not the least) their professional people have to operate".[181] A corollary of this approach would argue that with appropriate adjustments in its political economy, including macroeconomic policy changes, tax policy changes, educational revitalization and the like, the United States can reverse the currently adverse economic trends and shore up its "natural" status as unquestionably the single most important military, economic and political power. It could be argued, based on resurgent U.S. manufacturing exports and a drive to enhance U.S. global competitiveness by creating a North American Free Trade Area, that this process is already under way.

Scenario 1: Constructive globalization of Japan

One scenario for Japan's role, which might be styled the "good Japan", would have Japan interacting with Asia as an increasingly open economy, partially supplanting the United States as an export market for Asia-Pacific countries, while at the global level using its financial resources to undergird the present system. As an aid giver, Japan's horizons would expand to encompass more fully Africa, Latin America and the Third World debt. Its aid programmes would emphasize greater participation by non-Japanese firms and more emphasis on human resources development than large infrastructure activities. Its investment projects would involve more participation by local sub-contractors, transfer more technology, and be more oriented towards the Japanese market. Under this scenario, Japan would only marginally increase its military forces in consonance with greater "burden-sharing", while the United States and Japan would also continue to co-operate closely to meet mutually perceived security threats to the region and generally promote stability.

Scenario 1 more or less conforms to futures sketched out by internationally minded Japanese as well as Western analysts. At one end of the scale, it would parallel Takashi Inoguchi's "Pax America II", and at the other end concepts of U.S.-Japan power sharing such as Robert Gilpin's "*nichibei* [Japan-U.S.] economy", C. Fred Bergsten's "bigemony" or Zbigniew Brzezinski's "Amerippon". It could even be stretched to encompass the concept of a more pluralistic "Pax Consortius".[182] Regardless of the centre of gravity of the system, this scenario would see Japan more ambitiously using its growing economic power to support the current global trading system.

This scenario would appear to be most likely in an expanding global economy, which would make easier the pursuit of enlightened self-interest on the part of Japan, the United States and the NIEs. The viability of this scenario would seem to be dependent on the arguments of optimistic analysts that underlying factors in the world economy are favourable. These analysts emphasize trends such as the integration of global markets that is seen as producing a "third industrial revolution", demographic trends in the United States that in the future will

favour more savings and investment, and a trend towards gradual reduction of budget deficits in the industrialized countries.[183]

Scenario 1 would also appear more likely in a stable international
environment — in which Japan could continue to see its contribution
to stability primarily in economic terms — but also in an environment
in which Japan saw its security relationship with the United States
and the U.S. regional military role as still important to its interests.
Current trends towards Sino-Russian *détente* and the resolution of regional
disputes, coupled with continued Japanese awareness of a need for the
United States as a balancer, would seem to favour this scenario.

This scenario would follow from political and economic indicators
that Japan still seeks global partnership with the United States rather
than either a go-it-alone approach or isolation. Japan's commitment
to global partnership could well grow as the result of the selection of
Prime Minister Miyazawa, a leader with definite and well thought-out
views on Japan's international role, albeit tinged with nationalism.

The scenario conforms closely to recent policies. A July 1990 MITI
White Paper stressed Japan's need "to bring its domestic systems and
practices into better harmony with those of the rest of the world, and
increase their transparency". The overall thrust of the report stressed
the need for Japan to adjust its internal policies so as to enable it to
play a more interactive role in supporting an open global economic
system and strengthening Asia-Pacific co-operation.[184]

Despite mutual recriminations over Japan's response to the Gulf war,
the Kaifu government moved swiftly to try to restore close ties. During
a March 1991 visit to Washington, Foreign Minister Taro Nakayama
emphasized Japan's desire to play the role of a partner, not an "under-
ling".[185] Prime Minister Miyazawa has expressed in even more articulate
terms his view that although Japan does not possess the ability to assume
the posture of a global leader, it can and should share responsibility
with the United States for the management of the international system.

In the defence sphere, the 1990 Japanese Defense Agency annual
report found new reasons to cling to the U.S.-Japan security relationship despite the end of the Cold War.[186] Some argue, in fact, that
the re-emergence of the United States as "Number One" during the
Gulf war, U.S. successes in trade negotiations and other developments

have reasserted the familiar "clear hierarchy" with which the Japanese are most comfortable. As a consequence, it is asserted that "today both Americans and Japanese are settling back into the familiar partnership — with the United States as senior partner — that constitutes one of the most orderly aspects of the New World Order". As a result, despite enough trade and other conflicts "to keep platoons of negotiators crossing the Pacific ... the U.S.-Japan relationship is doing fine".[187]

Some might draw a quite different conclusion from the January 1992 visit of President George Bush to Japan, with the strong U.S. emphasis on trade complaints. On balance, however, the atmosphere and outcome of the visit still seem to reflect a continuing mutual commitment to economic interdependence and global partnership, at least at the official bilateral level.

Economically, this scenario would follow from the positive indicators of Japan's emergence as an increasingly important export market for Asian producers, and even for the United States. It likewise follows from indications that Japan is moving in the direction of relying more on its domestic economy than exports for sustaining its economic growth,[188] and for rapidly growing technological tie-ups and joint production arrangements between U.S. and Japanese high-technology firms.

An important theoretical basis for this scenario is the premise that Japan cannot suspend indefinitely the operation of what many see as universal economic laws. A number of Japanese analysts are firmly convinced that rising factor costs in Japan and growing competition from lower cost producers will force import liberalization, regardless of rearguard action by vested interests. Some would even argue that offshore investment, now viewed as "restructuring", will eventually create the same "hollowing-out" of the Japanese economy that occurred when U.S. multinationals began to shift manufacturing operations offshore to lower their costs and thus maintain their market shares in the 1960s and 1970s.

Some already see evidence of unrealistically inflated land and stock prices, and the weakening of the yen against the dollar during much of 1990 and 1991, and slowing growth as indicators that Japan's economic profile will soon look a lot more like that of other industrialized countries, including the United States. If this happens, the result could be a more balanced kind of regional economic interdependency, with the "division of labour" not so evidently tilted in Japan's favour.

In terms of Japan's international political role, the intellectual foundations of globalization are shaky, at best. Support in Japan for a more altruistic aid policy and for necessary measures such as macroeconomic policy co-ordination with the United States and other industrialized countries remains thin. Even here, positive Japanese responses may stem from a desire not to alienate the U.S. Administration or Congress or to "win points" with the United States and the West to offset economic friction.

The closest approximation of a globalization policy that has been developed in any detail is that articulated under the concepts of "comprehensive development" and the related New Aid Policy. In both of these, the balance between enlightened self-interest and economic nationalism is fragile and very subjective. The underlying concept of the New Aid Policy is just as capable, if not more so, of contributing to a Japan-dominated Asia-Pacific, as in scenario 3 below.

In security affairs, Japan's evident ongoing commitment to close co-operation with the United States must be weighed against evidence of rising impatience with the U.S. demands for increased burden sharing in the form of base support costs and a clamour from a minority of Japanese to "say no" to the United States. The FSX controversy, in which supporters of Japan's aerospace industry who favoured a go-it-alone approach to a new generation multi-role combat aircraft were pitted against those favouring joint development, appears to have provoked greater resentment of what is seen as U.S. dominance of the alliance, especially after the United States successfully insisted in 1989 on revising the terms of co-operation. American demands during the Persian Gulf war likewise provoked considerable resentment, even though the public ultimately supported the government's response by a narrow margin.

A Harris survey commissioned by the *Asahi Shimbun*, a leading daily newspaper, in May 1990 indicated that the percentage of Japanese who think that their country benefits from the U.S.-Japan security treaty had fallen to less than half — 48 per cent — during the survey period, a figure that is still high by historical standards. While the

Asahi Shimbun attributed the decline in support for the Alliance primarily as a result in developments in U.S.-Soviet relations and in Eastern Europe, it noted that some 40 per cent of the respondents now favoured the development of defence self-reliance "away from dependence on the United States", a symptom, in its view, of a phenomenon called "America *banare*", or "movement towards departure from the alliance".[189] Any significant progress in improving Japan-Russian relations will likely increase such sentiment among a substantial portion of the public.

Scenario 2: Heightened economic rivalry in Asia

A second scenario, which might be called the "bad Japan", sees Japanese aid and investment in Asia as primarily acting to increase the competitive position of Japanese companies in world markets *vis-à-vis* the fast rising NIEs, while Japan's own markets remain relatively closed. Under this scenario, Japan's ability to exercise positive influence in the Asia-Pacific region eventually would be sharply curtailed due to a lack of reciprocity in its relations with its neighbours. Over time, tensions between Japan and its Asian neighbours, as well as increasing strains in the U.S.-Japan relationship, could lead to the remilitarization of Japan and the decay of the current U.S.-led Asia-Pacific security system.

Scenario 2 could have ominous implications for all of the Asia-Pacific countries, as well as the United States, since it would call into question the continuity of the last two decades of steady and rapid economic growth. It would also bode ill for long term U.S. security interests in Asia and the Western Pacific due to the potential loss of forward basing access in Japan and the emergence of a new and probably unstable power balance.

A number of analysts see economic conflict at least as likely as co-operation in the Asia-Pacific region, though this is still a minority viewpoint. Some argue that factors such as the growing compression of the product cycle due to technological change and the increasing involvement of governments in directing industrial restructuring have deepened competition across the Pacific region rather than facilitated a more liberal trading environment or a "flying geese" style division of labour.[190]

A stalemate or breakdown in the GATT talks coupled with a continuation of the trend towards preferential regional trade zones as in EC 92 and NAFTA could be seen as heightening the competition between three economic blocs. According to analysts, Mexico's wage rates are lower than Singapore's and competitive with Malaysia, Thailand and China.[191] Some see U.S. firms as bolstering their global competitiveness by shifting low wage employment to Mexico, while their U.S. operations concentrate on higher value added activities, much as Japanese companies currently operate in Southeast Asia.

Scenario 2 could also be seen as following from Japan's "inability or unwillingness to restrain the one-sided and destructive expansion of its economic power",[192] coupled with a sharp contraction of the U.S. market either as a result of protectionism or a severe world-wide economic slowdown. One result could be the destruction of the post-war free trade system and the emergence of a bitter economic competition with the NIEs, especially as the would-be "new Japans" of South Korea and Taiwan compete with Japan for shares of a declining world market.

The thesis that Japan has not and will not significantly abandon its neo-mercantilist policies has for some time been garnering strong support in the United States. It is elementary to the writing of a diverse group of Japan-watchers such as Clyde Prestowitz, Karel van Wolferen, Chalmers Johnson, Ronald Morse and James Fallows, even though they differ on U.S. policy prescriptions. The thesis is also supported by data indicating that Japanese trade liberalization is still largely a function of industrial restructuring and adjustments in agricultural policy rather than a broader commitment to the principle of freer trade.

Some pessimists see Japan's economic policies as leading down the same road as its militarism and foolhardy expansionism in the 1930s.[193] Other factors that potentially could lead Japan into confrontation with its Asian neighbours include evidence of rising Japanese nationalism, which some see as already penetrating to the political centre.

The prospects for something like Scenario 2 would depend importantly on an eventual contraction of the U.S. market, possibly as a result of an abrupt adjustment to the current structural imbalances in the global economy. While governments, many private analysts, the IMF and OECD project favourable medium and long-term growth trends, others draw a more sober picture, emphasizing seemingly irresolvable problems such as the need for the United States not just to eliminate its huge trade deficit, as it nearly did in 1991, but to achieve a large surplus to cover accumulated interest obligations.[194]

One destabilizing source of adjustment might be a sharp rise in protectionism in the United States, perhaps mirrored in other countries whose balance of payments is also under extreme stress. Another source could be a discriminatory form of a North American Free Trade Agreement. If the NAFTA were structured to discriminate against third country manufacturing operations in Mexico, it could undercut the competitiveness of Japanese and other Asian goods in the U.S. market. One effect might be to greatly intensify competition among Asian countries along the lines of this scenario. Equally plausible, depending on Japan's stance, would be the solidification of sentiment in favour of a Japan-led Asian trade bloc, as in Scenario 3 below.

A May 1990 survey article on Japan's growing regional role in the *Far Eastern Economic Review* argued that "if U.S. imports shrink drastically over the next five years as a result of efforts to balance the federal budget, export-dependent newly industrialized countries (NICs) could be faced with a choice between promoting sales in the region or growing much more slowly". The article noted an analysis by the World Institute for Development-Economics Research that Japan's imports of Asian goods were "not likely to grow at anything like the rate needed to replace the U.S. as chief 'absorber' of Asian exports".[195]

Others have sketched out a bleak future if the United States decides that it is unwilling or unable to continue its post-war leadership role. To some, the abandonment of that role will cause the international political order to "collapse, taking the world trading system and the economic fortunes of the United States and its major allies along with it".[196]

The outcome of the move towards a more economically and politically integrated Europe in 1992, now partially under a cloud as a result of the reunification of Germany and other developments, will also have an important bearing on whether economic competition in the Asia-Pacific region remains an expanding sum situation, as at present, or a zero-sum economic rivalry. The strong redirection of Japanese exports from the United States to Europe and developments such as the brief tenure of a "Japan basher", Edith Cresson, as French Prime Minister, raise major questions about the future of Japanese access to the EC market and, consequently, about the openness of the global trading system. The erection of new barriers to trade could push the world either toward economic regionalism or destructive trade rivalry as in this scenario. To a lesser degree, the denial of Most Favoured Nation status to China by the United States, were it to come to pass, also has the potential to promote trade warfare with spillover effects on the Asia-Pacific region as a whole.

Other developments call this scenario into question. In terms of demonstrable economic realities, the kind of situation that would pit Japan in a ruinous competition with the NIEs for shrinking markets is not yet in evidence, although South Korea's current problems and its protectionist responses could be seen as presaging this scenario. First, expectations in Asia of a sharp decline in access to the American market are probably alarmist. American policy to date has emphasized foreign market opening strategies more than domestic protectionism, and imports from the region continue to grow with the significant exceptions of imports from South Korea, Taiwan and Hong Kong. Second, Japan's own relative dependence on exports for growth is rapidly declining despite the continued strong surge of its trade surplus.

The main argument against this scenario is that it may be too early to say that Japan will not substantially liberalize its trade policy in the future. Basic economic factors, combined with new developments such as consumer pressures for lower priced goods, could still be the beginning of a significant political change in the direction of a more open economy. After failing in the mid-1980s to overcome bureaucratic and business opposition, the policy argument for liberalization has received a new boost. In the debate over how to respond to the U.S. Structural Impediments Initiative, even the powerful Keidanren business association came down on the side of opening up the retail trade sector, as did much of the press. In terms of basic economic forces, while Japan is moving towards more complete dominance of certain high technology areas, and even regaining competitiveness in certain heavy industrial areas like steel, an underlying trend towards a progressive loss of comparative advantage in middle and lower technology areas continues.[197]

Scenario 3: Japan-dominated Asia-Pacific region

A third scenario sees Japanese aid and investment, and increasing access to the Japanese market by Asian exporters, as producing a Japan centred Asia-Pacific economy, even more pronounced than at present. Some might call this scenario the "real Japan", based on the view that Tokyo's policies remain excessively neo-mercantilist. Notwithstanding the pejorative implications of the scenario, it has the potential to be either a positive-sum or zero-sum situation. At one end of the scale, it can be viewed in positive terms as an extension of an ongoing shift of the centre of gravity of power in the Asia-Pacific region in the direction of Japan, in which the effects for most countries *besides* the United States would be not unlike scenario 1. At the other end of the scale, it could resemble a modern equivalent of the "Co-prosperity Sphere", where Japan's dominance had negative consequences for its neighbours due to a fundamentally inequitable economic and political order.

Under both variants of this scenario, Asia-Pacific countries would become increasingly dependent on Japan for capital flows (both aid and investment) and increasingly tied to Japan by trade links, while U.S. domestic manufacturers and multinationals would face increased competition from Japanese multinationals both in Asia and in the U.S. market. While this scenario could provide for continued dynamic economic growth in the region, the differentiation of functions between Japan and its neighbours would remain biased in favour of Japan, including a heavy dependence on Japanese-controlled technology. Over the longer term, Japanese political influence would expand at U.S. expense, while the U.S.-Japan security relationship would likely suffer from the effects of increasing trade friction and U.S. resentment at Japan's growing power.

The viability of this scenario as a positive-sum situation would depend on the ability of intra-Asian trade to become relatively self-sustaining, especially the ability of the Japanese market to supplant the United States as an engine of regional economic growth. The prospects of the NIEs to achieve developed country status and the hopes of the less developed countries (LDCs) to achieve NIE status may hang in the balance. The 1990 annual report of the Asian Development Bank, whose largest donor, Japan, exercises predominant influence over loan policy, stressed intra-Asian trade, in which Japan plays a central role, as the key to sustaining Asia-Pacific growth.[198] As noted above, other estimates of Japan's ability to supplant the U.S. market as an engine of Asia-Pacific growth are not so optimistic.

Emergence of a Japan-centred regional trade bloc?

Some already see the possible emergence of a Japan-centred regional trading bloc that will effectively freeze U.S. companies out of their "natural" level of participation in Asian growth. The available data are mixed, and the kind of data being offered in support of the regional trading bloc thesis could well prove not to have the expected result.

The realization of a Yen Bloc could result from either of two different developments. One possible source could be the development of trade blocs *outside* Asia leading to high Asian dependence on the Japanese market. Many in Asia have seen the U.S.-Canada Free Trade Zone, negotiations on a North American Free Trade Area, and the impending transition of the EC to a unified market as leading, ultimately, to rising barriers to Asian manufactures in North American and European markets. A *de facto* Yen Bloc could also result from the sheer weight of Japan's growing economic role in the region and a relative decline of the U.S. role compared to that of Japan.

While noting the still strong economic ties of Asian countries to the United States, Edward Lincoln argued in 1988 that just as the United States was moving in the direction of reducing its trade deficits, cutting its aid programmes, and reducing its overseas investment, Japan was moving in the direction of reducing its trade surpluses, boosting its aid and rapidly increasing its offshore investment. "As this situation develops," Lincoln argued, "the potential rises for Japan to offer a preferential Asian trading and investment zone which does not include the United States."[199]

Another factor pointing to a Japan-centred Asia is the strong lead that Japan still maintains in product-oriented research and development. Although South Korea and Taiwan in particular are rapidly increasing their R&D efforts, the total effort by the most advanced Asia-Pacific countries is less than one-twentienth that of Japan's.[200] Disparities in total GNP are similarly significant. At US$131.3 billion in 1987, South Korea's GNP was slightly over five per cent of Japan's US$2.3 *trillion* economic output. Even with twice the growth rate of Japan, the NIEs and ASEAN countries individually will remain relative pygmies, although their aggregate GNP will be significant and their trade impact could be even larger than Japan's since exports account for a much higher proportion of their national income.

The main argument against the Yen Bloc thesis is the simple fact that Japan's growing investment in the Asia-Pacific region is still aimed at the U.S. market to a large extent, and that any kind of a closed system would still appear to pale in comparison to the present trans-Pacific system. Even if intra-Asian trade and investment continues to accelerate, the United States likely will still loom as the most attractive single market both to Japan and to its Asia-Pacific neighbours. Thus far, U.S.-Japanese interdependence has been deepening rather than weakening, with increasing numbers of joint manufacturing and development ventures, and growing exports back to Japan of the output of Japanese transplant factories in the United States.

Given the still strong third market focus of Japanese and NIE investment in the Asia-Pacific region, a real Yen Bloc looks far more likely to develop as a result of the emergence of trade blocs elsewhere in the world. Among other things, a real as opposed to an informal Yen Bloc would require Japan to allow the yen to supplant the dollar as the medium of trade in the region. In addition, there is no evidence that Japan's economic managers have any desire to see their country replace the United States as the main market for regional exports. For Japan, a Yen Bloc still looks a distinctly less attractive option than an expanding world economy and a stable international environment within which the country can best grow and prosper.

For other reasons as well, Japan would seem to face an uphill struggle to convert its role as the "core economy" into full fledged regional economic and political dominance, let alone military sway. If Japan pushes too hard, the potential for an Asian backlash remains strong. Even now, the other militarily and industrially powerful Asian countries such as

China and South Korea are in no mood to accept a politico-economic replay of the 1930s. The less developed countries have shown time and time again that local forces of ethnic and political nationalism are strong enough to overwhelm neat calculations of national economic self-interest.

These limitations notwithstanding, the situation as of mid-1992 may suggest to some Japanese policymakers the attractiveness of an Asian card. While Japan appears clearly committed to APEC, its stance on the EAEG has been more equivocating, and different parts of the Japanese bureaucracy and body politic appear to have different views. Some apparently see the Mahathir proposal as a useful foil to a protectionist form of a North American trade zone. Other, more nationalistic Japanese seem to view a Japan-led bloc as an attractive alternative to the difficult task of managing global economic interdependence.

8
Implications for the future of the Asia-Pacific region

The foregoing analysis has considered the implications of Japan's expanding economic role and influence in the Asia-Pacific region from the perspective of the dynamic interaction of economic, political and security factors. The objective of the analysis was to gain a clearer picture of the systemic effects of the relative rise of Japan's role *vis-à-vis* the United States, and to develop alternative scenarios for Japan's future role in the region.

Any discussion of specific implications for the future structure of economic, political and security relationships in Asia and the Western Pacific, and for the interests of various Asia-Pacific countries and sub-regions is bound to be controversial. The following discussion is intended to suggest some tentative implications for the future of the region that would appear to follow from the foregoing analysis, within the stated frame of reference, i.e. the respective roles of the United States and Japan. A different frame of reference might yield an alternative or even competing set of implications.

Evolving dynamics of the Asia-Pacific region
Several basic generalizations concerning the roles of the United States and Japan in the changing dynamics of the Asia-Pacific region appear to follow from past experience and current trends.

First, it cannot be assumed that current power relationships in the Asia-Pacific region are immutable or that the nations of the region will continue to strike the same balance in their security and economic policies. The end of the Cold War has had significant impact on the political and security calculations of many countries in and outside the region, and has caused economic relations in many cases to be viewed in a new light. In particular, U.S. relations with Japan and other East Asian allies have come under strain due to trade friction and a weakening sense of shared security concerns.

Second, this revised relationship between economics and geopolitics appears to challenge some basic assumptions about the region's economic future. While Japanese offshore investment has strengthened a trend towards expanding intra-Asian trade, continuing Japanese import resistance, increasing U.S. formal and informal trade barriers, and other indications of economic nationalism appear to be fostering a counter-trend. Having lost their labour cost advantages and facing stiffer competition in their intermediate technology product lines, some of the NIEs may be at a crossroad. Recent developments such as "voluntary" action by South Koreans to remove Japanese, U.S. and European "luxury goods" from store shelves in response to an emerging trade deficit, for instance, could be interpreted as a straw in the wind that could presage the emergence of a more competitive rather than a more co-operative Asia-Pacific region.

Third, and related to the above, continuing strong obstacles to economic liberalization in Japan and the unique trade profile of the Japanese economy continue to raise troubling questions about the extent to which the Japanese market can replace that of the United States as an engine of growth for the region. While the Japanese economy can be expected to grow at a faster rate than the U.S. and other industrialized economies, and Japan's total imports may continue to grow strongly, the overall ratio of manufactured imports to GNP remains far lower than other industrialized countries. Most troubling is the fact that the rate of growth of manufactured imports from key Asia-Pacific trading partners such as the NIEs has been slowing down sharply since 1988 and became negative in 1990. The current slowdown in Japan's GNP growth rate could exacerbate this trend.

Fourth, while intra-Asian trade can be expected to continue to increase in importance, its potential for expansion cannot be taken for granted. To date, intra-Asian trade still appears heavily linked to trade outside the region, especially with the United States. Should the United States become more protectionist, the global economy stop growing, or Japanese offshore investment continue to fall it is questionable how much intra-Asian trade would continue to expand.

Finally, despite its preference for allowing the United States to take the lead in promoting stability and security in the Asia-Pacific region, Japan has shown an aversion to power vacuums and a willingness when necessary to employ its own economic power and political influence to promote stability and simultaneously enhance its commercial interests. This was apparent in the case of Japanese policy towards Southeast Asia after the U.S. withdrawal from Indochina, and concerns about stability were also evident in contemporary Japanese policies towards China and the Korean peninsula. The limitations of Japan's political system and the historical baggage of its role prior to and during World War II, however, make Japan ill-equipped to substitute for the United States as a stabilizing military power or a geopolitical balancer. On the contrary, should Japan become de-coupled from the American security relationship, any further growth in its military power would in itself be viewed with considerable discomfort by most, if not all, of its neighbours.

Implications for U.S. policy

The above generalizations suggest that unless Japan's growing role and influence develops within the framework of an open Asia-Pacific trading system and continuing close U.S.-Japan co-operation, it cannot help but have important negative economic and geopolitical consequences for the United States and the region as a whole. The United States faces a formidable task, however, in seeking to maintain or broaden the present open trading system in the Asia-Pacific region, and to promote a stable geopolitical balance, while adjusting to a shift of economic and financial power towards Japan and maintaining its own relevance to the region. A major task for U.S. policymakers will be to give greater credibility than heretofore has been the case regarding U.S. intentions

to remain an Asia-Pacific military power, or to indicate how it wishes
to see regional security relationships evolve in the event of a diminished
military role.

U.S.-Japan Relations

The United States has compelling reasons to come to terms with the
Japanese challenge in the Asia-Pacific region, but it has only recently
begun to address these issues in a systematic and co-ordinated fashion.
The Assistant Secretary for East Asian and Pacific Affairs, Richard H.
Solomon, addressed many of the foregoing themes in testimony before
the Senate Foreign Relations Committee on 17 May 1991. Solomon
called particular attention to the eclipse of the United States as an
aid donor to regional states by Japan, economic imbalances in U.S.
relations with Japan, and an emerging multi-polar security system,
coupled with growing interdependence. His statement, one of the more
comprehensive articulations of U.S. policy towards the Asia-Pacific
region in recent years, pointed to the need for "sustained engagement"
by the United States in the region and for not losing perspective on
the benefits of close U.S.-Japan relations, notwithstanding ongoing trade
friction.[201] The visits by President Bush and senior U.S. officials to
Japan and other Asia-Pacific countries in late 1991 and early 1992
appear aimed at heightening U.S. policy attention to the region, shoring
up U.S. bilateral relationships, and signalling stronger interest in APEC.

The obvious dilemma for the United States is that to regard Japan
as an emerging threat to U.S. well-being is potentially self-fulfilling
and will not necessarily solve some basic U.S. problems, while failing
to address the implications of Japan's emergence as the core economy
of the region could have significant economic and geopolitical consequences. Therein lies a conundrum: Japan's emergence as the economic
nerve centre of the region and its growing political influence may suggest
a continuing need for significant, offsetting, U.S. economic, political
and security involvement in the region, but the very factors that have
led to Japan's increasing prominence also tend to undercut congressional
and public support for bearing the costs of active U.S. involvement — i.e.

market openness, aid and military deployment costs. Despite a strong element of emerging rivalry, the United States and Japan retain a vital interest in co-operation. Japan's growing leadership in many areas of advanced technology, its geopolitical position and the extensive degree of industrial cross-investment among American and Japanese multi-national companies, all make Japan an attractive partner for the United States in the Asia-Pacific region.

Japan, for its part, still depends heavily on the U.S. market, has a major financial stake in the health of the U.S. economy, still needs a nuclear-armed ally against potential threats from the former U.S.S.R. and China, and has only limited ability to expand its influence in the Asian and the Western Pacific region except in the context of an overall political and security framework in which the United States is a major player (as at present).

The United States would appear to have a general interest in trying to move Japan in the direction of greater market openness and "global partnership", as in scenario 1, or at a minimum trying to limit the extent of Japanese dominance of the region, as in the least exclusivist version of scenario 3. Market openness and partnership in the region have long been the twin goals of U.S. policy, but the debate over how to achieve them has become increasingly divisive, notwithstanding a series of generally successful trade negotiations with Japan and other East Asian nations during the 1990–91 time frame.

A major cause of the acrimony over U.S. policy towards Japan has been a prevalent feeling that getting Japan's agreement to follow a path of enlightened self-interest may be less of a problem than obtaining actual results. While Japan's leaders may *officially* adopt globalist policies tending towards scenario 1, competition-minded Japanese businesses, and perhaps their allies at MITI, may behave in ways that tend to bring about scenario 2 or 3.[202] In some cases, U.S. disappointments may stem from outright failures of the Japanese Government to deliver on commitments, as in the case of an agreement on semiconductors. In other cases, the problem may stem from a failure to recognize the myriad Japanese ways of politely "saying no".

Macroeconomic policy co-ordination between Japan and the United States would seem an essential element of enhanced global partnership, as in scenario 1. A number of analysts have argued persuasively that the serious structural imbalances that developed in the 1980s occurred because the United States and Japan were pursuing mirror-image fiscal policies, the one emphasizing fiscal retrenchment, and the other deficit-financed expansion.[203] Some arguable gains were made in the Structural Impediments Initiative negotiations between the United States and Japan in mid-1990, including Tokyo's agreement to spend more on infrastructure projects, which *in theory* will raise capital costs, divert funds from research and development, and reduce the trade deficit via foreign participation in public works projects. To date, efforts at economic policy co-ordination through the G-7 meetings and bilateral negotiations have been politically difficult for both countries. In terms of the U.S. side of the equation, however, the general macroeconomic prescriptions to achieve better economic policy co-ordination are similar to those being recommended to enhance U.S. competitiveness, i.e. measures to increase savings and investment and reduce the budget deficit.

U.S. trade and foreign economic policy

Access to the U.S. market represents a major source of U.S. influence in the Asia-Pacific region, and is also a prime subject of domestic policy contention. Provided that U.S. policymakers do not actually have to employ the "stick" of trade retaliation, market opening initiatives aimed at Japan and other Asian trading partners would tend to support scenario 1. Actual retaliation, however, would tend to encourage heightened economic conflict, as in scenario 2, or excessive dependency of Asia-Pacific countries on Japan for their economic vitality, as in scenario 3.

From a foreign policy perspective, and arguably, from an economic policy perspective as well, measures to reduce the U.S. budget deficit and address other domestic problems of lagging competitiveness are preferable to market opening measures that require excessive bilateralism or the threat of protectionist trade retaliation to be effective. At the same time, many countries in the region applaud U.S. efforts to promote market opening in Japan. Some even support efforts to open up protected sectors in countries such as Taiwan, South Korea and the Asian developing countries so long as the spotlight is not turned in *their* direction.

The Bush Administration has, if anything, brought increased pressures to bear on Japan for trade reciprocity and created new spurs to co-operation from both Japan and the EC under the Uruguay Round of the GATT. "Fast track" negotiations on a North America Free Trade Agreement promise not only to make the United States more competitive but also carry an implied threat to resort to "blocism" should Europe and Japan fail to co-operate on agricultural reform and other matters in the GATT.[204] ·

Export and foreign investment promotion policies

The surge of Japanese aid and investment into Southeast Asia raises some potentially serious questions about the future climate for U.S. business and exports. Will the greater openness of Asian developing countries to foreign investment ultimately benefit all players or only Japan and the NIEs? Is the stagnation of U.S. investment in the Asia-Pacific region related to a sense that the Japanese already have locked up the markets, or is it just a counterpart to the comparatively low level of U.S. domestic investment?

Thus far, the main causes of lagging U.S. direct investment in the Asia-Pacific region would appear to lie in the same structure of incentives and disincentives that have caused an overall tendency towards low domestic savings and investment, and perhaps the greater attractiveness of domestic investment as a consequence of high capacity utilization and strong export growth during the 1988–90 time frame. It is arguable whether there is an a priori case for measures to promote U.S. foreign investment since economists disagree strongly about whether foreign investment harms or benefits domestic economic welfare, whatever its effect on U.S. foreign and security policy interests. On the other hand, there is a strong possibility that the failure of U.S. firms to invest more in the Asia-Pacific region, combined with growing Japanese sectoral dominance, will leave American companies and U.S.-owned multinationals out of what currently is the fastest growing region of the world.

Last but not least, the United States has the option to "fight fire with fire" as in a plan implemented in mid-1990 to provide US$500 million in credit through the U.S. Export-Import Bank and the U.S. Agency for International Development to finance sales of American telecommunications, transportation, power and construction equipment to the "spoiled markets" of Indonesia, Thailand, the Philippines and Pakistan. Earlier, in 1986, Congress had given the U.S. Export-Import Bank a "war chest" of US$300 million intended to serve as an incentive to dissuade other OECD countries from using tied aid to promote capital goods exports, an effort that thus far has had little or no success. Congress extended the availability of US$300 million in tied aid credits through FY 1991 in Public Law 101–240, signed into law in December 1989.

The idea has received a further boost in legislation introduced in late 1990 by Senators Max Baucus, Lloyd Bentsen, David Boren and Robert Byrd, entitled the Aid for Trade Act of 1990, parts of which have been incorporated in Title XI of a pending foreign assistance authorization bill for FY 1992–93, under the rubric "Aid, Trade and Competitiveness". As it came out of the House-Senate Conference to resolve differences, the bill would establish a "capital projects office" within the Agency for International Development (AID) which would work with the regional bureaus of AID, the Export-Import Bank and the Trade Development Agency to develop a strategy for assisting capital and infrastructure projects in Eastern Europe and developing countries. The bill would also require the Secretary of the Treasury and the President of the Export-Import Bank to report to Congress should negotiations with OECD countries to reduce tied aid fail by 1 February 1992. Finally, the bill also urges the President to "use at least $650 million in fiscal year 1992 and $700 million in fiscal year 1993 for capital projects".[205]

On the surface, export credits are a form of economic nationalism that tend to promote scenario 2, heightened economic competition, rather than scenario 1. Linking aid to exports also would reverse a more than two-decade long U.S. movement away from bilateral tied aid and subsidized exports. At the same time, tied aid can be seen as a logical response to Japan's New Aid Plan strategy, and hence an antidote to scenario 3, a Japan-dominated Asia. The idea may have more economic merit as a spur to reduce the "tied" element of other countries' aid programmes, since export subsidies by their nature distort trade. It would also seem to require a reorientation of U.S. aid priorities or the provision of additional resources, since in terms of going head-to-head with Japan's New Aid Plan, Japan has deeper pockets and the U.S. "fire" may be seen as short on fuel.

Greater aid co-operation with Japan

An alternative way to combat Japan's use of aid as an export tool and promote a scenario 1 outcome would be to put more pressure on Japan to change its own ways. The United States would appear to have a compelling interest in joining with other donors to pressure Japan to reduce the commercial aspects of its aid programme. One goal would be to get Japan to replace its present "request" based aid process with a programmatic one with more emphasis on basic development programmes such as education, sanitation, and health care, rather than to emphasize capital goods-intensive infrastructure projects. Another appropriate policy goal might be to seek a greater co-operation with Japan on rural and human development projects that would combine recognized U.S. expertise with Japanese financial resources.

Some aspects of Japan's New Aid Plan, such as the emphasis on hybrid official and private aid flows, would have much to commend them if in practice they were less self-serving. In terms of the U.S.-Japan aid dialogue, however, U.S. interests and those of the aid recipients in avoiding a scenario 3 outcome would be best served by pressure on Japan to enlarge the participation of local and third country suppliers in its aid projects.

To date, little of substance has been achieved in meetings between U.S. and Japanese aid officials. Basic problems include still largely incompatible aid strategies and objectives, and the inability of each country's bureaucracies to come to the table with definite bargaining positions. Existing trends suggest a tendency towards competition rather than co-operation in bilateral aid ventures.

U.S. regional security role

American policymakers will have to weigh the costs and benefits of maintaining an active military presence in the Western Pacific, taking into account both budgetary and foreign policy considerations, as well as the willingness of Asian countries to host U.S. forces. Whatever decisions the United States makes, it seems clear that for a variety of reasons Japan will remain fundamentally unequipped to replace the United States as a stabilizing military power. While international and regional political conditions could make a major U.S. military presence increasingly redundant, an equally likely prospect is that a sharp cutback in U.S. forces would set off destabilizing reverberations.

From this perspective, a U.S. cutback would tend to promote the multiplication of military power centres, and hence scenario 2, or, less likely, an eventual attempt by Japan to assert a military as well as economic "Pax Nipponica", as in one variant of scenario 3. In the event of a significant reduction in the U.S. military role, a tendency towards scenario 2 looks more likely than scenario 3 for two broad reasons. First, the number of regional military powers is growing already. The list of regional powers includes India and Japan, at the extremities of the region, the two Koreas and Taiwan, as well as established powers such as Vietnam and China. Most of them have the capability to build and deploy nuclear weapons, and some of them have a growing incentive to do so. Second, Asian countries remain hostile to any repetition of Japanese military dominance, including some like the Soviet Union and China who could do something about it.

At present the signs appear favourable for a continued U.S. military role in the region, albeit with an adjustment of responsibilities between the United States and its allies. The Bush Administration has recognized the new uncertainties arising out of the end of the Cold War and indicated its desire to adjust the U.S. forward deployments "in ways that sustain our defenses and those of our allies — yet in ways that will forge more mature patterns of responsibility sharing".[206] Tokyo's agreement to provide more support costs for U.S. forces in Japan, and the post-Gulf war prestige of the U.S. military would appear to be favourable straws in the wind. However, should the perception grow among the public and Congress that the U.S. stake in Asia is marginal, or that Japan benefits inordinately from its dominant economic position, Japanese concessions regarding burden sharing may prove inadequate to offset the diminished U.S. domestic support base for military deployments in Asia.

Implications for Asia-Pacific nations

Stake and responsibility for shaping the future

The Asia-Pacific nations have benefited greatly from the same factors that have led to the current structural imbalances in U.S. trade with them. While many Asia-Pacific nations can take credit for having made the right policy decisions to attract foreign investment and promote exports, most of the rapid growth in their exports and national income during the 1980s was the direct result of the massive U.S. trade deficits.

Given the evident necessity to redress the imbalances in U.S. trade with Asia-Pacific nations, which were unsustainable at levels experienced in the 1980s, the Asia-Pacific nations including Japan have a vital stake in promoting a smooth transition to a more stable situation. The transition is already under way. Since 1985, the growth of U.S. exports to the region have substantially exceeded the still strong import growth. As of early 1991, the United States had moved into a situation of surplus with all of the NIEs except Taiwan, and the Japanese trade surplus had fallen about 20 per cent to around US$40 billion.

Further movement towards balance will require additional steps both in the United States and by Japan and the other Asia-Pacific countries.

First and foremost, both exports to Japan and intra-Asian trade must continue to expand if the region is to adjust smoothly to a relative decline in the role of the U.S. market as an engine of growth. This will require a new outlook among regional states regarding market openness, especially among the NIEs and the fast growing ASEAN countries, which have benefited most from the dynamic 1980s.

Second, new levels of political and security co-operation, formal or informal, would be helpful in making sure that the end of the Cold War does not lead to a new period of instability as a result of the emergence of multiple power centres or the re-emergence of historical sources of conflict and rivalry. On the plus side, the ASEAN countries and Japan have already made considerable strides in effectively damping down the destabilizing effects of the Cambodian conflict, even if the bitter and seemingly insolvable conflict itself has not completely ended. On the negative side, there is plenty of evidence that the potential for regional instability remains and, particularly in the security sphere, ASEAN has had difficulty in defining its rationale. Big question marks surround the future role of China in Southeast Asia and the stability of the Korean peninsula.

Institutionalizing Asia-Pacific economic co-operation?

In terms of their shared interests in the structure of economic, political and security relations in the Asia-Pacific region, both the United States and the countries of the region have a vital stake in the form that any future institutionalization of Asia-Pacific economic co-operation may take. The now unlikely emergence of a forum without U.S. participation would decidedly favour Japanese domination of the region, as in scenario 3. Questions remain about the participation of China, Taiwan and Hong Kong, for reasons peculiar to their special relationship.

Concern that the U.S. maintain a leadership position in the Asia-Pacific region appears to have been one reason why Secretary of State James Baker announced at a 26 June 1989 speech to the Asia Society, in New York, that the United States was interested in Australian Prime Minister Hawke's proposal for a new pan-Pacific economic entity to expand trade and promote a multilateral approach to mutual concerns. This policy decision played a major role in facilitating the Canberra ministerial meeting on Asia-Pacific Economic Cooperation. As expected, despite other policy distractions the United States showed revitalized commitment to APEC during Secretary of State Baker's attendance at the November 1991 ministerial meeting at Seoul, where the United States also reiterated its objections to the Malaysian East Asia Economic Group (EAEG) plan.

The further institutionalization of Asia-Pacific economic co-operation would appear to have certain clear benefits for the United States and all of the Asia-Pacific economies:

• It would give Japan an important forum for playing a role in shaping future economic relationships and promoting its own ideas of complementarity, but also a commitment to "good citizenship", thus promoting scenario 1.
• It could facilitate a co-operative approach to dealing with the current structural imbalances (i.e. the U.S. trade deficit and the Japanese/NIEs surpluses) which still endanger the future growth of the region.
• It would give the Asia-Pacific nations the ability not only to seek common approaches in international negotiations such as the current Uruguay Round of the GATT, but also a forum in which to seek to influence the stances of the United States and Japan as well as a vehicle for gaining leverage with the European Community.

At the same time, the interests and concerns of the United States, Japan, and other important Asia-Pacific economic powers differ in a number of important respects. Both Tokyo and Washington also have had internal policy conflicts that prevented them from taking clear positions on APEC or taking strong steps to advance the discussions. In addition, the other Asia-Pacific countries remain divided, as evidenced by reaction to Prime Minister Mahathir's proposal for an East Asia Economic Group.

As of late 1991, it appears that Washington and Tokyo may be prepared to give additional policy attention to Asian economic co-operation. Three factors in particular appear to be stimulating stronger U.S. interest. These include favourable trends in U.S. trade with the region; eagerness to dispel fears that movement towards a North American Free Trade Area might be viewed as anti-Asian; and concern about the implications of Mahathir's EAEG proposal.[207]

Japan, for its part, has serious concerns about matters such as the possible adoption of restrictive local content thresholds that might be incorporated in the NAFTA covering third country investment in Mexico. Partially in response, MITI appears to have adopted a two-pronged regional bloc strategy. On the one hand, it has cautiously backed a watered-down version of the EAEG — probably calculated as striking a balance between getting the attention of the United States without imposing unwanted responsibility on itself as the "core economy" and main alternative market for Asian exports. Meanwhile, Japan reportedly seeks to accelerate progress towards institutionalizing APEC and engaging the United States in broad discussions about regional trade issues, thereby countering unwanted North American exclusivity.[208]

Conclusions

On balance, it appears that while Japan will become the economically dominant power in the Asia-Pacific region, Tokyo's ability to expand its influence at the expense of the United States will probably be constrained by conflicting domestic political interests and Asian opposition to a Japanese security role. None the less, U.S. economic and other interests may be diminished by the widespread Asian perception that the United States is preoccupied with North American and European concerns and is withdrawing from the Asia-Pacific region.

Despite continued resistance to imports by vested interests, a number of economic factors are undercutting Japan's comparative advantages in certain medium technology areas, while forces for economic liberalization appear at this time gradually to be gaining strength. Under the best of circumstances, however, it remains questionable whether Japan will open its market enough, and whether the potential market is absolutely large enough, to be a credible alternative to the U.S. market. The possibility of self-sustaining growth in the Asia-Pacific region, especially with greater Japanese market openness, is plausible but by no means assured. Asian countries can be expected to resist Japanese concepts of the appropriate economic "division of labour". Japan has as yet shown itself unwilling or unable to give any overall sense of direction or co-ordination to its aid programmes or to exercise much more than behind-the-scenes political influence.

Given the factional and still relatively parochial nature of Japanese politics, it is doubtful whether Tokyo can actually assume political leadership in proportion to its economic power. Japan is changing in the direction of a more globalist perspective, but the process is painfully slow. While Japan's ongoing defence buildup and the possible sharp reduction in the U.S. military presence in the region could make Japan the strongest regional military power after Russia and China, no Asian country welcomes a Japanese security role and important powers like China are positively hostile to a militarily strong Japan. The rapid growth of intra-Asian economic interaction and the movement towards a more multipolar geopolitical environment seem all the more to require new forms of dialogue and co-operation in order to maintain growth and stability and forestall adverse scenarios.

The main threat to the interests of all of the countries of the Asia-Pacific region would appear more likely to come indirectly from a general breakdown of the present economic and security framework than directly from the displacement of U.S. influence or the rise of Japan's. While Japan's economic power and influence are indeed growing, and partly at the expense of the United States, the latter retains important options and a large measure of control over its own future. Other important Asia-Pacific nations also enjoy strong enough economies and freedom of action to have important influence over their own destinies and the prospects for the region as a whole. Whether they will exercise their political and policy management options wisely, or act in ways counter-productive to their own long term interests and those of the region, is a question of the highest urgency.

Appendices

Comparisons of foreign direct investment (FDI) should be regarded with great caution. Some argue that they should not be used at all due to significantly differing methodologies. An analysis of methodological problems suggests that overall comparisons are, at a minimum, less useful than measurements of the trends — which in most data sources show recent Japanese investment increasing at a rapid rate while U.S. investment in the Asia-Pacific region has been relatively stagnant during the past decade, especially as measured in constant dollars.

Japanese FDI data is based on notifications to the Japanese Government of intent to carry out investment approved by the host government, whereas U.S. data from the Department of Commerce's *Survey of Current Business* is based on estimated capital flows and equity positions of U.S. firms and foreign affiliates. Thus Japanese data tends to be anticipatory and the methodology tends to overstate Japanese investment when compared to U.S. investment as measured by the more conservative U.S. method. Host government estimates, which often are based on approvals of proposed investment, tend to overstate both Japanese and U.S. investment.

In what is probably an extreme case of understating U.S. investment compared with Japanese FDI, the U.S. Commerce Department valued

U.S. investment in the People's Republic of China (PRC) as of 1988 at only US$310 million, versus US$2.6 billion in approved investment estimated by the Chinese Government. (Recent disinvestment in China has brought U.S. equity down to under US$300 million.) On the other hand, the Japanese Ministry of Finance estimate of US$2 billion in cumulative notified Japanese FDI as of 31 March 1989 is nearly the same as the Chinese estimate of US$2.1 billion.

Recipient countries vary widely in how they track foreign investment. Hong Kong doesn't keep overall data on foreign investment but conducts an annual voluntary survey on manufacturing investment — by admission an incomplete and imprecise process. The U.S. *Survey of Current Business* shows US$594 million invested in *manufacturing* in Hong Kong as of 1988, versus an original cost estimate of US$1.1 billion shown by the Hong Kong Government's annual report. Japanese data similarly underestimates investment by about half compared to the Hong Kong survey data — i.e. Japanese Ministry of Finance data shows US$0.5 billion invested in manufacturing in Hong Kong as of 1988 versus US$0.9 billion estimated by the Hong Kong Government.

While it may be safe to assume that the PRC and Hong Kong are atypical cases, individual country data tends to underscore the fact that if U.S. and Japanese cumulative investment were measured on the same basis, they would be somewhat closer to being equal. In terms of new investment, it seems much clearer that Japan is outdistancing the United States, though the extent of the gap is open to argument.

For a particularly scathing attack on FDI comparisons, see a paper by Eric D. Ramstetter of Kansai University, Osaka, "An Overview of Multinational Firms in Asia-Pacific Developing Economies: An Introduction to the Commonplace Ignorance", prepared for the Asian Productivity Organization/Institute for Economic Development and Policy Seminar on the Role of Foreign Direct Investment in Development, held in Seoul, Korea, 16–20 September 1991.

Appendix B
Japanese trade with Asia-Pacific countries, 1986–90
(In US$ millions)

	Imports						Exports					
	1986	1987	1988	1989	1990	% Change 1986–90	1986	1987	1988	1989	1990	% Change 1986–90
NIES	12,608	19,027	25,014	27,137	25,944	105.8	30,286	39,804	49,820	52,756	56,688	87.2
Hong Kong	1,080	1,577	2,111	2,215	2,172	101.1	7,214	8,947	11,708	11,528	13,080	81.3
Singapore	1,475	2,081	2,338	2,953	3,576	142.5	4,612	6,064	8,312	9,240	10,716	132.4
South Korea	5,334	8,172	11,827	12,997	11,712	119.6	10,558	13,344	15,443	16,565	17,460	65.4
Taiwan	4,720	7,198	8,738	8,969	8,484	79.8	7,902	11,449	14,357	15,422	15,432	95.3
ASEAN (4)	14,009	16,505	18,997	21,792	24,408	74.2	7,548	9,614	13,020	16,646	22,188	194.0
Indonesia	7,386	8,500	9,493	11,016	12,708	72.1	2,682	3,016	3,055	3,301	5,040	87.9
Malaysia	3,986	4,814	4,709	5,124	5,400	35.5	1,723	2,188	3,061	4,124	5,508	219.6
Philippines	1,235	1,375	2,041	2,063	2,148	74.0	1,098	1,429	1,740	2,381	2,508	128.4
Thailand	1,402	1,816	2,754	3,589	4,152	196.2	2,045	2,982	5,164	6,840	9,132	346.6
Non-Market	5,980	7,864	10,379	11,780	12,924	116.1	10,312	8,734	9,914	8,888	6,528	-36.7
China (PRC)	5,726	7,478	9,860	11,140	12,024	110.0	9,936	8,336	9,482	8,522	6,132	-38.3
North Korea	169	240	323	295	300	77.3	185	216	239	197	180	-2.6
Vietnam	84	145	196	346	600	614.3	191	181	193	169	216	13.2
South Asia	1,664	2,042	2,359	2,563	2,616	57.2	3,030	2,921	3,209	3,047	2,712	-10.5
India	1,309	1,546	1,806	1,974	2,076	58.6	2,119	1,976	2,083	2,018	1,704	-19.6
Pakistan	355	497	553	589	540	52.0	911	944	1,126	1,028	1,008	10.7

Appendix B (Continued)

	Imports						Exports					
	1986	1987	1988	1989	1990	% Change 1986–90	1986	1987	1988	1989	1990	% Change 1986–90
Other Asia	1,578	1,388	1,471	1,458	1,632	3.4	1,247	1,111	1,069	1,087	1,164	−6.6
Oceania	8,429	9,718	12,780	14,167	14,748	75.0	7,066	6,919	8,368	9,974	8,964	26.9
Australia	7,046	7,974	10,285	11,566	12,324	75.0	5,274	5,196	6,684	7,806	6,900	30.8
New Zealand	964	1,180	1,645	1,658	1,728	79.3	1,114	1,138	1,040	1,348	1,212	8.8
Pacific Islands	419	564	850	943	696	66.2	678	586	643	821	852	25.7
Total Asia-Pacific	44,268	56,544	71,000	78,898	82,272	85.9	59,488	69,103	85,400	92,399	98,244	65.2
Reference Comparison												
U.S.	29,407	31,957	42,295	48,520	52,728	79.3	81,886	84,992	90,264	93,718	90,888	11.0
Canada	4,936	6,109	8,300	8,653	8,376	69.7	5,570	5,662	6,426	6,806	6,732	20.9
OECD-Europe	18,342	22,860	30,512	35,198	42,708	132.8	37,862	46,116	56,124	56,602	63,396	67.4

NOTE: Numbers may not add due to rounding.

SOURCE: OECD Monthly Statistics on Trade.

Appendix C
U.S. trade with Asia-Pacific countries, 1986–90
(In US$ millions)

	Imports					% Change	Exports					% Change
	1986	1987	1988	1989	1990	1986–90	1986	1987	1988	1989	1990	1986–90
NIES	46,136	57,664	63,232	62,756	60,492	31.1	18,290	23,546	34,880	38,458	40,740	122.7
Hong Kong	8,891	9,854	10,243	9,739	9,492	6.8	3,030	3,983	5,690	6,304	6,840	125.7
Singapore	4,726	6,200	7,996	8,950	9,840	108.2	3,380	4,052	5,770	7,352	8,016	137.1
South Korea	12,730	16,987	20,189	19,742	18,492	45.3	6,355	8,099	11,290	13,478	14,400	126.6
Taiwan	19,790	24,622	24,804	24,325	22,668	14.5	5,525	7,412	12,131	11,323	11,484	107.9
ASEAN (4)	9,452	10,798	12,800	15,728	17,268	82.7	4,974	5,807	7,040	8,630	10,776	116.6
Indonesia	3,312	3,394	3,188	3,542	3,324	.36	946	767	1,056	1,256	1,896	100.5
Malaysia	2,420	2,921	3,712	4,745	5,268	117.7	1,729	1,896	2,140	2,875	3,420	97.8
Philippines	1,973	2,263	2,682	3,064	3,384	71.5	1,363	1,600	1,880	2,207	2,472	81.3
Thailand	1,747	2,220	3,218	4,378	5,292	202.9	936	1,544	1,964	2,292	2,988	219.2
Non-Market	4,771	6,294	8,513	11,988	15,228	219.2	3,137	3,521	5,054	5,818	4,824	53.8
China (PRC)	4,771	6,294	8,513	11,988	15,228	219.2	3,107	3,497	5,039	5,807	4,812	54.9
North Korea	—	—	—	—	—	—	—	—	—	—	—	—
Vietnam	—	—	—	—	—	—	30	24	16	11	.012	−60.0
South Asia	2,609	2,933	3,413	3,838	3,804	45.8	2,366	2,197	3,592	3,599	3,624	53.1
India	2,284	2,528	2,952	3,314	3,192	39.8	1,536	1,464	2,498	2,464	2,484	61.7
Pakistan	325	404	461	523	612	88.2	830	733	1,093	1,135	1,140	37.3

Appendix C (Continued)

	Imports						Exports					
	1986	1987	1988	1989	1990	% Change 1986–90	1986	1987	1988	1989	1990	% Change 1986–90
Other Asia	1,099	1,379	1,458	1,691	2,016	83.4	468	445	548	521	516	10.3
Oceania	3,718	4,135	4,823	5,273	5,772	55.3	6,659	6,526	8,243	9,848	9,972	49.8
Australia	2,632	3,007	3,532	3,900	4,440	68.7	5,551	5,495	6,983	8,348	8,544	53.9
New Zealand	983	1,051	1,183	1,231	1,224	24.5	881	818	943	1,118	1,140	29.4
Pacific Islands	103	77	108	142	108	4.7	227	212	317	382	288	27.1
Total Asia-Pacific	67,786	83,202	94,238	101,274	104,580	54.3	35,894	42,042	59,358	66,874	70,452	96.3
Reference Comparison												
Japan	81,911	84,575	89,802	93,586	89,652	9.5	26,881	28,249	37,732	44,584	48,588	80.8
Canada	68,252	71,084	80,921	88,210	91,368	33.9	45,332	59,814	69,233	78,266	82,968	83.0
OECD-Europe	89,130	94,636	99,520	100,817	108,132	21.3	61,003	69,090	87,187	99,722	112,224	84.1

NOTE: Numbers may not add due to rounding.
SOURCE: OECD Monthly Statistics on Trade.

Notes

1. As used here, "Asia" includes South Asia, Southeast Asia, China and Northeast Asia. "Asia-Pacific" refers to these areas plus Australasia and the Pacific Islands (also shown as "Oceania" in some data presentations). The term "Asia-Pacific region" as used here is distinct from the term "Pacific Rim". The latter refers to the whole Pacific basin, including the littoral states of the Western hemisphere, but not necessarily all of Asia, i.e. the "Pacific Rim" does not customarily include South Asia (the Indian subcontinent).
2. For an example of this line of analysis, see Mike Mansfield, "The U.S. and Japan: Sharing Our Destinies", *Foreign Affairs*, Spring 1989, pp. 3–15. Likewise, a planning document for FY 1988–92 adopted by the Japanese Cabinet in May 1988 emphasizes both the growth of Japan's economic power and its continued need for "conditions of international peace and a sound relational climate with sustained and stable growth in the world economy", in "Economic Management Within a Global Context" (Government of Japan, Economic Planning Agency), p. 1.
3. Poll data cited in "America and Japan: How We See Each Other. A Report Prepared for the Commission on U.S.-Japan Relations for the Twenty-First Century". Summary Overview reproduced in *Bulletin of the Japan-America Society of Washington* (Summer 1990): 2.
4. Steven R. Weisman, "Japanese Coin a Word for Feeling About U.S.", *New York Times*, 16 October 1991, p. A14.
5. *Asahi Shimbun*, 29 May 1990. Also cited in Reuters report in the *Straits Times*, 31 May 1990, p. 4.

6. Weisman, op. cit., *New York Times*, 16 October 1991, p. A14.
7. See for example, *The Economist*, 15 July 1989; *Far Eastern Economic Review (FEER)*, 29 September 1988, pp. 24–30; and the *Christian Science Monitor*, 6 November 1989, pp. 10–11; 13 November, pp. 10–11; 14 November, pp. 3–4; and 27 November, pp. 10–11.
8. Don Oberdorfer, "Looking East: Is America Losing its Clout in Asia?", *Washington Post*, 30 June 1991, p. C3.
9. Jeffrey E. Garten, "Asia and the New Economic Order", *FEER*, 11 April 1991, p. 54.
10. Asian Development Bank (ADB), *Asian Development Outlook, 1991* (Manila: ADB, 1990), p. 43. The data covers Japan and 17 Member Developing Countries of the Asian Development Bank, spanning South, Southeast and East Asia, as well as six Pacific Island countries.
11. Maria Luz Y. Baguiro, "ASEAN Aims to Boost Intra-Group Trade", *Nikkei Weekly* (Tokyo), 12 October 1991, p. 20.
12. See Takashi Inoguchi, "The Political Economy of Pacific Dynamism", in "Japan's Growing External Assets: A Medium for Regional Growth?" (Proceedings and Papers of ASEAN-China-Hong Kong Forum 1988, Centre for Asian Pacific Studies, Hong Kong, 1989), p. 67.
13. Prepared Statement of Edward J. Lincoln, Senior Fellow, The Brooking Institution, in U.S. House of Representatives, Committee on Ways and Means, *East Asia: Challenges for U.S. Economic and Security Interests in the 1990's* (Washington: U.S. Government Printing Office, 26 September 1988), p. 35.
14. At a meeting at the Plaza Hotel in New York in September 1985, the five leading industrial powers agreed on a realignment of the value of the yen against the U.S. dollar.
15. Kenneth S. Courtis, "Pacific Trade Imbalance to Expand Again", *Japan Times* (Weekly International Edition), 20–26 May 1991, p. 11.
16. Enlarging host country and *third country* [emphasis added] market shares was also mentioned in 66.2 per cent of the responses, another indication that such investment aimed at making Japanese firms more competitive (multiple motivations allowed). By way of contrast, the goal of reducing labour costs was cited in only 5.9 per cent of the responses for businesses investing in North America, while gaining market shares was cited by 76.5 per cent and acquiring technology by 32.4 per cent. These responses indicate that avoiding protectionism and enhancing qualitative competitiveness were the primary motivations for investment in the United States. Japan Development Bank, "Deepened International Linkages Among

Pacific Rim Countries: Trade, Foreign Direct Investment and Technology Transfer", no. 138 (February 1990): Table III-20, p. 105. Report is in Japanese.

17. Based on data in a Japanese Government "White Paper on Small and Medium-Sized Enterprises" and reproduced in a paper by Yoshihiko Miyauchi at a conference on The Future of Asia/Pacific Economic Relations in Hong Kong, 5–7 November 1989 (sponsored by the U.S. Asia Society and other international sponsors). The 1988 data is from a draft 1990 JETRO white paper on world foreign direct investment, obtained from their Tokyo office in March 1990 (p. 15 of the draft).

18. Paul A. Summerville, "Japan's Trade Surplus Again Shooting Up as Imports Wane, Exports to Asia Surge", *Japan Economic Journal*, 4 May 1991, p. 8.

19. Japan, Ministry of Foreign Affairs, *Japan's Official Development Assistance: 1990 Annual Report* (Tokyo: 1991).

20. Ministry of Foreign Affairs, Japan Brief 141, 6 October 1991, "Japan's ODA 1991 (White Paper on ODA): New Challenges and Tasks for Japan's ODA". [English summary of overview distributed by the Japanese Embassy in Washington.]

21. Robert M. Orr, Jr., "The Rising Sum: What Makes Japan Give?", *International Economy*, September–October 1989, p. 83. This assertion is difficult to validate strictly in terms of bilateral ODA flows, but it may be close to the mark taking into account Japan's contributions to multilateral lending agencies. In the case of Indonesia, for instance, Japan's bilateral loans and grants, along with Export-Import Bank credits, totalled about US$2 billion for FY 1988–89, or the equivalent of about 38 per cent of Indonesia's *development* budget expenditures for that year of about US$5.3 billion and all of its US$1.9 billion balance of payments deficit. Taking into account Japan's contributions to the Asian Development Bank, the World Bank and the IMF, Japan's contribution to financing Indonesia's total budget of about US$17.2 billion might approach 15 per cent. OECD, *Geographical Distribution of Financial Flows to Developing Countries*, 1985/1988 (Paris: 1990), pp. 152–53; and U.S. Department of Commerce, *Foreign Economic Trends and Their Implications for the United States; Indonesia*, May 1990, p. 2. (source for budget expenditure data.)

22. World Bank data cited in *FEER*, 29 September 1988, p. 25.

23. Al Nakajima, "Japan Cautiously Backs ASEAN Forum", *Nikkei Weekly*, 19 October 1991, p. 3.

24. Comparative investment levels should be regarded with caution, due to different methods of comparison and fiscal (Japanese) versus calendar year (U.S.) measurements. See Appendix A.

25. Data from the U.S. Institute for International Education (IIE), District of Columbia and New York, as published in the *Chronicle of Higher Education*, 28 November 1990, p. 11.

26. Japan Development Bank, "Deepened International Linkages Among Pacific Countries", op. cit., Tables IV-5, p. 134, and IV-10, p. 151.

27. Merrill Lynch Asian Economic Commentary quoted by the *Straits Times*, 12 October 1989, p. 40.

28. *FEER*, 28 March 1991, p. 50. These figures underscore once again the limitations of available investment data, since Japanese Ministry of Finance data shows US$673 million invested in Malaysia in the year ending 31 March 1990 on an approvals and notification basis. Presumably the higher numbers refer to asset value, rather than equity, but the data inconsistencies are troubling.

29. *FEER*, 28 March 1991, p. 50.

30. *FEER*, 27 September 1990, p. 58, and 28 March 1991, p. 50.

31. Based on a press report on a book by Gordon Redding, of Hong Kong University. *Business Times* (Singapore), 24–25 March 1990.

32. Kunio Yoshihara, *The Rise of Ersatz Capitalism in South-East Asia* (Singapore: Oxford University Press, 1988), pp. 3–4.

33. Interview with Nagatoshi Suzuki, Institute of Developing Economies (Tokyo), 22 March 1990.

34. *International Herald Tribune*, 3 May 1990, pp. 13, 19.

35. For an explicit description of Japan's apparent ambitions to "co-ordinate" production in Asia, see Bernard Wysocki, Jr., "Guiding Hand: In Asia, the Japanese Hope to 'Coordinate' What Nations Produce", *Wall Street Journal*, 20 August 1990, pp. A1, A2.

36. Dr Okita has credited the "flying geese" concept to Professor Kaname Akamatsu, who first formulated it in the 1930s. Saburo Okita, "Asian-Pacific Prospects and Problems: For the Further Development of the Asian-Pacific Cooperative Framework", paper prepared for In Search of a New Order in Asia, an International Symposium sponsored by the Institute of East Asian Studies at the University of California at Berkeley, and Dong A Ilbo, Seoul, 1–3 February 1990, p. 1.

37. Okita, "Asian-Pacific Prospects and Problems", op. cit., p. 2.

38. Masaharu Hanazaki, "Industrial and Trade Structures and the International Competitiveness of Asia's Newly Industrializing Economies — a Search

for Development in Harmony with the Industrialized Countries", Japan Development Bank Research Report No. 15, August 1989, pp. 1–2, 107.

39. The same caveats apply as in earlier discussions of investment comparisons. See Appendix A.

40. Al Nakajima, "Japan Under Pressure Over Asian Trade Surpluses", *Nikkei Weekly*, 17 August 1991, pp. 1, 13.

41. Robert Delfs, "Japan in Asia; Part 8: China", *FEER*, 25 April 1991, p. 52.

42. Jon Choy, "The Changing Pattern of Japanese Trade: Northeast Asia", *Japan Economic Institute (JEI) Report*, no. 31A, 14 August 1987, p. 7.

43. How much it is ahead of the United States is impossible to judge. According to an unclassified report by the American Consulate in Hong Kong, entitled "Foreign Investments in China: A Comparison of Hong Kong, Japanese and U.S. Strategies" (December 1989), the Chinese Government had approved US$2.6 billion in U.S. investment. The U.S. Commerce Department values U.S. equity at a radically lower, and declining, figure of US$289 million. A recent article on the efforts of Occidental Petroleum to dispose of its investment in a coal mine in China indicated that the value of Occidental's investments alone amounted to some US$250 million, but these probably reflect asset value, not equity (*New York Times*, 25 April 1991, pp. D1, 7). See Appendix A.

44. Japan Economic Institute (Washington, D.C.), *JEI Report*, no. 14B, 12 April 1991, pp. 4–5.

45. *FEER*, 22 August 1991, p. 10.

46. *Japan Economic Journal*, 23 March 1991, p. 14, and Japan Economic Institute, *JEI Report*, no. 14B, 12 April 1991, pp. 5–6.

47. *Straits Times*, 1 May 1990, p. 1.

48. This view was expressed in an Indian business journal article on Prime Minister Gandhi's April 1988 visit to Tokyo which noted "... if aid (with or without strings attached) is any consideration, the Japanese monolith is waiting on an aid-fattened India before deciding to bite". *Business India*, 15 May 1988, p. 57.

49. *Business India*, 15 May 1989, p. 58.

50. Japan, Ministry of Foreign Affairs, *Japan's Official Development Assistance: 1990 Annual Report*, op. cit.; U.S. Agency for International Development, "Congressional Presentation Volume for FY 1992", Main Volume, p. 220.

51. For a discussion of Japan's aid programmes in the South Pacific, see Alan Rix, "Japan's Foreign Aid Policy: A Capacity for Leadership?", *Pacific Affairs*, Winter 1989–90, pp. 461–75.

52. Japan, Ministry of Finance; U.S. Department of Commerce, *Survey of Current Business*, August 1989, Table 44, p. 95.
53. Robert M. Orr, Jr., "The Rising Sum: What Makes Japan Give?", *International Economy*, September–October 1989, p. 82.
54. *FEER*, 27 September 1990, p. 57.
55. U.S. Department of State, *Philippines: 1989-90 MAI Projects/Programs*, 1 May 1990; *FEER*, 7 March 1991, p. 53. The U.S. share excludes bases-related assistance.
56. Survey, "The Yen Block", *The Economist*, 15 July 1989, p. 12.
57. *The Economist*, 15 July 1989, p. 13; and Terutomo Ozawa, *Recycling Japan's Surpluses for Developing Countries* (Paris: OECD Development Centre, 1989), pp. 101–07.
58. "The Money Dumpers", *FEER*, 5 April 1990, pp. 46–47.
59. An April 1990 article in the *FEER* stated that a pending report by Japan's Overseas Economic Cooperation Fund (OECF) warned the Malaysian Government, which had received more than US$2.9 billion in loans and grants from Japan's OECF through 1988, that power interruptions and other indicators of infrastructure bottlenecks were jeopardizing Malaysia's prospects for new Japanese investment. *FEER*, 5 April 1990, pp. 46–47.
60. Robert M. Orr, Jr., "The Rising Sun: Japan's Foreign Aid to ASEAN, the Pacific Basin and the Republic of Korea", *Journal of International Affairs*, Summer/Fall 1987, pp. 39–62.
61. Robert M. Orr, Jr., "From the Land of the Rising Sun: The Private Sector and Japanese Official Development Assistance", *Hotel Okura News* (Tokyo) 14, no. 2 (February 1990): 1, 3; and Orr, "Collaboration or Conflict? Foreign Aid and U.S.-Japan Relations", *Pacific Affairs*, Winter 1989–90, pp. 476–89.
62. For instance, the U.S. Export-Import Bank provided US$60 million in soft loans to aid AT&T in winning a matching award to supply another 350,000-line digital switching system. *FEER*, 22 November 1990, p. 60.
63. Steve Coll, "Japan's Hands-On Foreign Aid", *Washington Post*, 13 January 1991, pp. H1, H3; *FEER*, 22 November 1990, p. 60.
64. *Washington Post*, ibid.
65. See Chapter II, "Issues Surrounding Japanese Aid and Characteristics of Japan's Aid", in Ministry of Foreign Affairs, *Japan's Official Development Assistance: 1990 Annual Report*, op. cit., pp. 18–24.
66. Embassy of Japan, Washington, D.C., "Japan's ODA 1991 (White Paper on ODA): New Challenges and Tasks for Japan's ODA", op. cit., p. 4.

67. Ministry of Foreign Affairs, *Japan's ODA: 1990 Annual Report*, op. cit., p. 21.
68. U.S. Department of Commerce, *Survey of Current Business*, August 1991, Table 17.
69. Kenneth S. Courtis, "Japanese Direct Foreign Investment to Expand: No 1990s Slowdown in Sight", *Japan Times* (Weekly International Edition), 2–8 September 1991, p. 6.
70. *FEER*, 3 May 1990, p. 49.
71. *FEER*, 27 June 1991, pp. 16–17.
72. Doug Tsuruoka, "Look East and Up; Malaysia Embraces Japan as its Economic Model", *FEER*, 28 March 1991, pp. 50–51.
73. Adam Schwarz, "Price of Security: Japan's Aid to Indonesia Reflects Strategic Concerns", *FEER*, 27 September 1990, pp. 56–58.
74. *International Herald Tribune*, 30 May 1990, pp. 1, 21.
75. M. Hadi Soesastro, "Southeast Asia's Expectations of Japan with Respect to Investment" (Paper delivered at the Japan-Southeast Asia (JASA) Conference, Kuala Lumpur, Malaysia, 24–27 November 1989), p. 15.
76. *FEER*, 3 May 1990, p. 48.
77. Policy Speech by Prime Minister Toshiki Kaifu, Singapore, 3 May 1991, entitled "Japan and ASEAN: Seeking a Mature Relationship for the New Age". Provisional translation supplied by Japanese Embassy, Washington, D.C..
78. The same asymmetry between Japan's economic and commercial success and lack of political acumen that marks Tokyo's regional diplomacy today was remarked on over two decades ago in terms remarkably similar to current reactions. See, for instance, the evaluation of Asian trips conducted by Prime Minister Sato and Foreign Minister Miki in 1967 in Hans H. Baerwald, "Japan: New Diplomatic Horizons, Old-Style Domestic Politics", Asian Survey, January 1968, pp. 43–45, and reaction to Prime Minister Kaifu's April–May 1991 ASEAN tour in a 13–19 May 1991 article in the *Japan Times* (Weekly International Edition) entitled "Kaifu's Trip Shows Aid Outshines Political Clout".
79. Alan Rix, "Japan's Foreign Aid Policy: A Capacity for Leadership?", op. cit., pp. 466–67.
80. Sueo Sudo, "Japan-ASEAN Relations: New Dimensions in Japanese Foreign Policy", *Asian Survey*, May 1988, pp. 512–16.
81. Ibid., p. 512.

82. Comprehensive National Security Study Group, "Report on Comprehensive National Security" (tentative translation), submitted to Acting Prime Minister Masayoshi Ito, 2 July 1980, pp. 1–2, 14–16.
83. *Straits Times*, 1 May 1989, p. 1.
84. K.V. Kesavan, "Japan and the Tiananmen Square Incident: Aspects of the Bilateral Relationship", *Asian Survey*, July 1990, p. 673.
85. *New York Times*, 28 January 1990, p. 8.
86. Bertil Lintner, "Reward for Resistance", *FEER*, 24 October 1991, p. 10.
87. *FEER*, 11 April 1991, p. 45.
88. Ibid., p. 587.
89. See for instance, Takashi Oka, "Burma's Tears", *Christian Science Monitor*, 24 May 1991, p. 19. Oka notes that pressure on Burmese leaders could only succeed if simultaneous pressure is put on the regime's "principal neighbors and economic partners — China and Thailand".
90. Juichi Inada, "Aid to Vietnam: Japan's Policy", *Indochina Report* (Singapore), July–September 1989, pp. 1–7.
91. Mary Kay Magistad, "Japanese Getting Ready for Opening of Vietnamese Market", *Washington Post*, 2 January 1991, pp. D1, 2; and Akihiro Tamiya, "Japanese Firms Eager to Tap Potential of Socialist E. Asia", *Japan Economic Journal*, 10 November 1990, p. 5.
92. Donald S. Zagoria, "The Great Powers and Indochina", in *The Challenge of Indochina: An Examination of the U.S. Role; April 19–21, 1991*, edited by Dick Clark, pp. 34–35 (Queenstown, MD: The Aspen Institute, 1991).
93. Hisao Takagi and Gwen Robinson, "After Gulf, Japan Focuses Diplomacy on Cambodia", *Japan Economic Journal*, 23 March 1991, pp. 1, 4.
94. Donald S. Zagoria, "The Great Powers and Indochina", in *The Challenge of Indochina: An Examination of the U.S. Role; April 19–21, 1991*, op. cit., p. 35.
95. "Waiting in The Wings; Japan in Asia: Part 10: Vietnam", *FEER*, 30 May 1991, p. 68.
96. Nobuyuki Oishi, "Japan Companies Ready to Develop Cambodia at First Sign of Peace", *Japan Economic Journal*, 25 May 1991, pp. 1, 30.
97. *Japan Times* (Weekly International Edition), 20–26 May 1991, p. 3.
98. *Japan Times* (Weekly International Edition), 21–27 January 1991, pp. 1, 5.
99. Japan Economic Institute (Washington), *JEI Report*, no. 46B, 7 December 1990, p. 7.
100. Japan Economic Institute (Washington), *JEI Report*, no. 8B, 1 March 1991, p. 7.

101. Ministry of Foreign Affairs, *Japan's ODA: 1990 Annual Report*, op. cit., p. 174.
102. Larry A. Niksch, "The Philippines", in *Japan-U.S. Relations: A Briefing Book*, edited by Richard P. Cronin, CRS Report for Congress, No. 91-401F (Washington: Congressional Research Service, Library of Congress, 1 April 1991), p. 80.
103. Larry A. Niksch, "The Philippines", op. cit.
104. *FEER*, 3 May 1990, p. 49.
105. *Japan Economic Journal*, 4 May 1991, p. 4.
106. "Ministries play rivals as Japan seeks active role", *Straits Times*, 4 November 1989, p. 32.
107. Ibid.
108. Off the record interviews in June 1990 with diplomats who attended the sessions.
109. *Straits Times*, 31 March 1990, p. 11.
110. Agence France Presse (AFP) report, published in the *Straits Times*, 16 April 1990, p. 12.
111. *FEER*, 28 March 1991, p. 51.
112. Takashi Inoguchi, "Four Japanese Scenarios for the Future", *International Affairs* (Tokyo), Winter 1988/89, p. 15.
113. "Japan Builds a New Power Base: Its Emerging Clout in East Asia Could Come at America's Expense", *Business Week*, 10 April 1989, p. 42.
114. Saburo Okita, "Managing the Japan-U.S. Relationship" (unpublished paper), June 1989, p. 3.
115. Straits Times (Singapore), 10 May 1990, p. 15.
116. "Kaifu's Trip Shows Aid Outshines Political Clout", *Japan Times*, 13-19 May 1991, pp. 1, 3.
117. While conceding that Japan could not remain "aloof" from impending changes in the strategic landscape in East and Southeast Asia, the editorial criticized reported Thai suggestions of a naval co-operation and a Malaysian suggestion that appeared to welcome a larger non-military role for the Soviet Union as "without well-prepared reasoning". *Jakarta Post*, 7 May 1990, p. 6.
118. Gwen Robinson, "Hun Sen Visit Raises Question of Japan Role Regarding Cambodia", *Japan Economic Journal*, 4 May 1991, p. 3.
119. Karel van Wolferen, *The Enigma of Japanese Power*, (New York: Alfred A. Knopf, 1989) pp. 41-43.
120. Interview by R. Taggart Murphy in the *New York Times*, 2 April 1989.

121. *Tokyo Shimbun*, 21 August 1991 (English translation published in U.S. *Foreign Broadcast Information Service [FBIS]*, East Asia, Daily Report, 26 August 1991).

122. Hisao Takagi, "Foreign Ministry Blamed for Gulf Crisis Policy Gaffe: Diplomats Reply, Citing Weak National Leadership", *Nikkei Weekly*, 22 June 1991, p. 1.

123. Doug Tsuruoka, "Look East, and Up", *FEER*, 28 March 1991, p. 50.

124. Japan Institute for Social and Economic Affairs, *Japan, 1990: An International Comparison*, Table 10-7, p. 82.

125. Based on interviews conducted in Japan with Japanese Government officials and business leaders in December 1988.

126. Ministry of Foreign Affairs, *Japan's Official Development Assistance: 1990 Annual Report*, op. cit., p. 15, 143-45.

127. *Jakarta Post*, 7 May 1990, p. 1.

128. *FEER*, 1 September 1988, p. 47.

129. *Indian Express*, 4 April 1989, pp. 1, 9.

130. *Straits Times*, 3 May 1990. Singh's comment may have been more aimed at the United States, which had been pressing New Delhi to remove its 40 per cent foreign equity limit on foreign investment by naming India under the "Super 301" provisions of the U.S. 1988 Trade Act. The government headed by Prime Minister Narasimha Rao has now raised the limit to 51 per cent and significantly opened up the Indian market.

131. *FEER*, 2 May 1991, pp. 36-37.

132. *FEER*, 10 March 1988, pp. 69-70.

133. *FEER*, 3 May 1990, pp. 49-52.

134. See Kit G. Machado, "Japanese Transnational Corporations in Malaysia's State Sponsored Heavy Industrialization Drive: The HICOM Automobile and Steel Projects", *Pacific Affairs*, Winter 1989-90, pp. 504-33.

135. David E. Sanger, "A New Car for Malaysia, New Influence for Japan", *New York Times*, 6 March 1961, pp. D1, D6.

136. *Straits Times*, 6 February 1990, p. 1.

137. Assessment based on interviews with government officials, policy analysts, businessmen and academics in a number of Asian countries including India, Indonesia, Singapore and Thailand during late 1989 and early 1990. This theme also runs through the *FEER's* "Japan in Asia" series cited at various points in this book.

138. Remarks attributed to Chandra Muzaffar, president of Aliran, in a "Japan in Asia" series article on Malaysia. *FEER*, 28 March 1991, p. 54.

139. See for instance, Hirokazu Shiode, "The Ugly Japanese in Asia", *Journal of Commerce*, 23 August 1989, p. 8A, and *FEER*, 3 May 1990, p. 50.
140. Richard Baum, "China in 1985: The Greening of the Revolution", *Asian Survey*, January 1986, pp. 51–52.
141. Stanley Rosen, "China in 1986: A Year of Consolidation", *Asian Survey*, January 1987, pp. 52–53.
142. Michael Richardson, "In Australia, Setbacks for a 'Super City'", *International Herald Tribune*, 4 April 1990, p. 8.
143. Michael Vatikiotis, "The Gentle Giant: Kaifu Soothes Fears Over Japan's Political Plans", *FEER*, 16 May 1991, pp. 16–17.
144. *Straits Times*, 16 May 1990, p. 28.
145. *Japan Times*, op. cit., 13–19 May 1991, pp. 1, 3.
146. *Japan Times* (Weekly International Edition), 8–14 July 1991, p. 4.
147. *New York Times*, 10 October 1991, p. A3.
148. David E. Sanger, "A New Car For Malaysia, New Influence for Japan", op. cit.
149. Bruce Stokes, "Making Eyes at Moscow", *National Journal*, 20 January 1990, pp. 116–19.
150. Defense Agency, *Defense of Japan, 1990* [English translation] (Tokyo: Japan Times Ltd., 1991), pp. 3, 90–97.
151. *Defense of Japan, 1990*, op. cit., Table 3–7, p. 167.
152. Charles Smith, "Constitutional Cover", *FEER*, 13 September 1990, pp. 16–17; Richard Katz, "U.S. Hopes Ozawa Will Continue to Play Strong Role", *Japan Economic Journal* (Weekly), 20 April 1991, p. 3.
153. Louise do Rosario, "Attacked on All Fronts", *FEER*, 7 March 1991, pp. 26–27.
154. *The Economist*, 9 March 1991, pp. 32–33.
155. Larry A. Niksch, "Japan–U.S. Relations in the 1990s", CRS Report for Congress No. 89–264 F, 7 April 1989, pp. 7–13; and Gary K. Reynolds, "Japan's Military Buildup: Goals and Accomplishments," CRS Report No. 89–68 F, 27 January 1989.
156. Tokyo *Kyodo* in English, 30 September 1991 (reproduced in *FBIS*, East Asia, Daily Report, 1 October 1991, p. 3)
157. Steven K. Vogel, "Japanese High Technology, Politics, and Power". Berkeley Roundtable on the International Economy, Research Paper No. 2. Berkeley, CA, March 1989, pp. 1, 3.
158. Vogel, "Japanese High Technology, Politics and Power", op cit., p. 3.
159. Harold Brown, "The United States and Japan: High Tech is Foreign

Policy", *School of Advanced International Studies (SAIS) Review*, Summer–Fall 1989, p. 2.

160. From Akio Morita and Shintaro Ishihara, *The Japan that Can Say "No": The New U.S.-Japan Relations Card*. Sony Corporation Chairman Akio Morita has disassociated himself from Ishihara's more anti-U.S. remarks and declined to allow an authorized English printing of the book. For one of many critical articles, see Michael Hedges and Valerie Richardson, "Book Gives Fodder to Japan-Bashers", *Washington Times*, 2 November 1989, pp. A1, A6.

161. The above discussion is based primarily on Michael Green, "Kokusanka: FSX and Japan's Search for Autonomous Defense Production" (Cambridge: Massachusetts Institute of Technology Japan Program, MITJP 90–09, 1990), pp. 3–8.

162. Ibid., pp. 43–54.

163. Ibid., pp. 54–57.

164. Michael Vatikiotis, "Assessing the Threat: Differences Over Priorities Negate Military Cooperation", [series of ASEAN focus articles] *FEER*, 20 June 1991, p. 29.

165. Gwen Robinson, "Japan Academies Open Doors to Foreign Military", *Nikkei Weekly*, 29 June 1991, pp. 1, 31.

166. "A Hesitant Patroller of the Pacific", *The Economist*, 27 July 1991, pp. 29–30.

167. Ayako Doi and Kim Willenson, "Japan: Back to the Past? The Idea of a 'Co-Prosperity Sphere' — Again", *Washington Post*, 11 August 1991, pp. C1, C4.

168. See articles by Koji Kakizawa, director of the National Defense Division of the LDP and a member of the Diet, and Tatsuro Kunugi, previously U.N. Assistant Secretary General, in the "Opinion" section of the *Japan Times* (Weekly International Edition), 29 April–5 May 1991, p. 11, and 8–14 July 1991, p. 11.

169. Hisao Takagi, "Japan to Seek Asian Security Meetings", *Nikkei Weekly*, 27 July 1991, p. 2.

170. Ayako Doi and Kim Willenson, "Japan: Back to the Past? The Idea of a 'Co-Prosperity Sphere' — Again", op. cit.

171. Ibid., p. C4.

172. Michael Vatikiotis, "Diety to Diplomat: Erstwhile Conqueror Searches for a New Regional Role", *FEER*, 3 October 1991, p. 38.

173. Russell Marshall, "Altered Perceptions", *FEER*, 28 September 1991, p. 36.

174. For some thinking about how Japan might gradually increase informal military ties with Southeast Asian countries, see Sueo Sudo, "Japan-ASEAN Relations: New Dimensions in Japanese Foreign Policy", op. cit, pp. 509–25.

175. *Straits Times*, 7 May 1990, p. 14. Commentators speculated that Chatichai was seeking a greater Japanese naval role in the region as an alternative counterweight to China. Chatichai is widely perceived as moving consciously to utilize Japanese support as leverage in an effort to steer Thailand into a role as the dominant economic power on the Southeast Asian mainland and the gateway for the future development of Indochina.

176. "A Hesitant Patroller of the Pacific", *The Economist*, 27 July 1991, pp. 29–30.

177. Government of Australia, *Australia's Regional Security*; Ministerial Statement by Senator the Hon. Gareth Evans QC, Minister for Foreign Affairs and Trade. Canberra, December 1989, pp. 5–6.

178. *Straits Times*, 9 January 1990, p. 1. (Reuter press service report)

179. Especially Inoguchi, "Four Japanese Scenarios for the Future", op. cit.

180. Some, such as Professor Rudiger Dronbusch of MIT argue that "in the end, world politics will set the pattern for trade and payment flows", and that Japan is "far too small" to claim the place now held by the United States. *Washington Post*, 16 July 1989, pp. B1, 2.

181. Susan Strange, "The Persistent Myth of Lost Hegemony", *International Organization*, Autumn 1987, p. 565.

182. See Inoguchi, "Four Scenarios for the Future", op. cit., pp. 20–23.

183. See Charles R. Morris, "The Coming Global Boom", *Atlantic Monthly*, October 1989, pp. 51–58, 62–64.

184. MITI, "International Trade and Industrial Policy in the 1990s — Toward Creating Human Values in the Global Area", (summary), 5 July 1990. p. 42.

185. Barbara Wanner, "Tokyo Strives to 'Reactivate' US-Japan Relations", Japan Economic Institute, *JEI Report*, No. 12B, 29 March 1991, pp. 7–9.

186. *Defense of Japan, 1990*, op. cit.

187. T.R. Reid, "Japan-Basking: New Pacific Era?; From Trade to Aid, Washington and Tokyo are Pursuing the Same Ends", *Washington Post*, 16 June 1991, pp. B1, B4.

188. In 1984, Japan's total GNP growth rate of 5.1 per cent was dominated by exports, which contributed 1.3 per cent of total growth. In 1988, a

total growth rate of 5.1 per cent resulted from a 6.8 per cent growth in domestic demand and a minus 1.7 per cent decline in external demand. Japan Institute for Social and Economic Affairs, *Japan 1990: An International Comparison*, Second Edition (Tokyo: 30 April 1991), Table 1–8, p. 10.

189. *Asahi Shimbun*, 29 May 1990. I am grateful to an anonymous reviewer for providing a precise clarification of the survey phraseology, *"amerika ni tayorazu, dukuji no boeitaisei o tsukuriageru bekida"*. Support for the U.S.-Japan security treaty dropped as low as 34 per cent in the wake of the 1971 "Nixon shocks" and remained at below 50 per cent until after the Soviet invasion of Afghanistan.

190. Chung-in Moon, "Conclusion: A Dissenting View on the Pacific Future", in *Pacific Dynamics: The International Politics of Industrial Change*, edited by Stephan Haggard and Chung-in Moon (Boulder, CA: Center for International Studies, Inha University, South Korea, and Westview Press, 1989), pp. 360–61.

191. *Washington Post*, 5 May 1991, pp. H1, H6.

192. James Fallows, "Containing Japan", *Atlantic Monthly*, May 1989, p. 41.

193. Murray Sayle, "The Powers That Might Be: Japan Is No Sure Bet As Top Dog", *FEER*, 4 August 1988, pp. 38–43. Cited in Takashi Inoguchi, "Four Japanese Scenarios for the Future", op. cit., p. 15.

194. Jeffrey E. Garten, "Japan and Germany: American Concerns", *Foreign Affairs*, Winter 1989/90, pp. 90–91.

195. *FEER*, 3 May 1990, pp. 46–47. The article contains a wildly erroneous statement that "U.S. imports from ASEAN, China, Taiwan and South Korea totalled US$54.4 billion, *six times* [emphasis added] Japanese imports from these countries." See Appendices B and C for a comparison of the actual figures, which show a ratio of about 3:2 of U.S. and Japanese imports from the countries in question.

196. Remarks of Aaron L. Friedberg at a September 1989 CRS Seminar on U.S. Power in a Changing World. U.S. Congress, House of Representatives, Committee on Foreign Affairs. *U.S. Power in a Changing World: Proceedings of a Seminar Held by the Congressional Research Service — September 19–20, 1989*; Report Prepared for the Subcommittee on International Economic Policy and Trade of the Committee on Foreign Affairs, U.S. House of Representatives, by the Congressional Research Service, Library of Congress. 101st Cong., 2nd Sess. (Washington: U.S. Government Printing Office, May 1990), p. 8.

197. One Japanese analyst argues that "the coefficient of Japan's trade special-
     ization with the NIEs and ASEAN moved toward zero in 1985–88 with
     regard to chemical products, iron and steel, metal products, general
     machinery, electric equipment and appliances and precision machinery".
     In other words, in these product areas Japan is moving towards a situa-
     tion where it is as likely to be a buyer as a seller. He further notes
     that "the coefficient during that period moved toward minus as far
     as products with high labour intensity . . . are concerned", meaning
     that Japan had already lost its comparative advantage. Chuji Kikutani,
     "Dynamic Development", *Journal of Japanese Trade and Industry*, no. 6
     (1989): 13.
198. "Intra-Asian Trade Building New Power Block in World Economy",
     Straits Times, 1 May 1990, p. 32. (Reuter news service report)
199. Prepared Statement of Edward J. Lincoln, Senior Fellow, the Brookings
     Institution, in U.S. House of Representatives, Committee on Ways and
     Means. "East Asia: Challenges for U.S. Economic and Security Interests
     in the 1990's", op. cit., pp. 38–39.
200. Based on a table in a Japanese Development Bank Report produced
     under the supervision of Masaharu Hanazaki, "Deepened International
     Linkages Among Pacific Rim Countries: Trade, Foreign Direct Invest-
     ment and Technology Transfer" (in Japanese), op. cit. The table compares
     the latest available R&D expenditures of Japan, the United States, Canada
     and eight Asian countries. Data years vary from 1984 to 1987 (United
     States and Japan), p. 124.
201. Richard H. Solomon, Assistant Secretary for East Asian and Pacific
     Affairs, "US Relations with East Asia and the Pacific: A New Era;
     Statement before the East Asian and Pacific Affairs Subcommittee of
     the Senate Foreign Relations Committee, Washington, D.C., May 17,
     1991", U.S. Department of State, Bureau of Public Affairs, *Dispatch*,
     Washington, 27 May 1991, pp. 383–90.
202. This potential dichotomy between official policy and firm behaviour
     was pointed out by Professor Paul Kennedy, of Yale University, in a
     comment on an early draft of this book.
203. This argument is a central theme of Edward J. Lincoln's book, *Japan
     Facing Economic Maturity* (Washington: The Brookings Institution, 1987).
204. *The Economist*, 20 April 1991, p. 11.
205. U.S. Congress, House of Representatives, International Cooperation Act
     of 1991; Conference Report to Accompany H.R. 2508, ordered to be

printed 27 September 1991, 102d Congress, 1st session, Report 102–225, Washington, DC., U.S. Govt. Print. Off., 1991, pp. 415–16.

206. Statement of Assistant Secretary for East Asian and Pacific Affairs, Richard H. Solomon, 17 May 1991, Department of State, *Dispatch*, op. cit., p. 384.

207. All of these factors were noted, directly or indirectly, in the Assistant Secretary of State's 17 May 1991 testimony before the Senate Foreign Relations Committee, op. cit.

208. Al Nakajima, "Japan Cautiously Backs ASEAN Forum", *Nikkei Weekly*, 19 October 1991, p. 3.

THE AUTHOR

Richard P. Cronin is a specialist in Asian Affairs with the Foreign Affairs and National Defense Division of the Congressional Research Service (CRS), a non-partisan research and information arm of the U.S. Congress. Dr Cronin has written a large number of CRS reports, articles and book chapters on Asian issues of U.S. policy concern, including the Afghanistan conflict, nuclear proliferation in South Asia, and U.S. security policy in Asia. Since becoming a division specialist in 1988, he has undertaken research on the issues of Japan's role in the changing political economy of Asia, and the implications of the shift of global economic and financial power towards Japan and the Pacific rim countries.

In addition to this book, his research resulted in a September 1990 CRS report for Congress entitled "Japan's Expanding Role and Influence in the Asia Pacific Region: Implications for U.S. Interests and Policy". He also wrote a related article on "A Japan Dominated Asia-Pacific Region?" in a Joint Economic Committee Compendium on Japan, published in December 1990, and an article entitled "Changing Dynamics of Japan's Interaction with Southeast Asia", in *Southeast Asian Affairs 1991*.